POPE FRANCIS

MICHAEL J. RUSZALA

About Wyatt North Publishing

Starting out with just one writer, Wyatt North Publishing has expanded to include writers from across the country. Our writers include college professors, religious theologians, and historians.

Wyatt North Publishing provides high quality, perfectly formatted, original books.

Send us an email and we will personally respond within 24 hours! As a boutique publishing company we put our readers first and never respond with canned or automated emails. Send us an email at hello@WyattNorth.com, and you can visit us at www.WyattNorth.com.

About the Author

Michael J. Ruszala holds an M.A. in Theology & Christian Ministry and a B.A. in Philosophy and Theology *summa cum laude* from Franciscan University of Steubenville and is certified as a parish catechetical leader by the Diocese of Buffalo. He is director of faith formation at St. Pius X Catholic Church in Getzville, NY, and an adjunct lecturer in religious studies at Niagara University in Lewiston, NY. Michael is also an active member of the Society of Catholic Social Scientists and serves on the Catechumenate Board and the Faith Formation Assessment Committee for the Diocese of Buffalo. He has been published in several religious journals including the Social Justice Review, the Catholic Social Science Review, and Lay Witness online edition, with articles often touching on contemporary papal teaching. With interests in music, art, tennis, and kayaking, he also enjoys directing the Children's Choir at his parish.

Foreword

Understanding the life of Jorge Mario Bergoglio is essential to understanding how Pope Francis shepherds his flock - and the key is mercy.

What exactly do people find so attractive about Pope Francis? There is something about him that captivates and delights people, even people who hardly know anything about him.

Aldo Cagnoli, a layman who developed a friendship with the Pope when he was serving as a cardinal, shares the following: "The greatness of the man, in my humble opinion lies not in building walls or seeking refuge behind his wisdom and office, but rather in dealing with everyone judiciously, respectfully, and with humility, being willing to learn at any moment of life; that is what Father Bergoglio means to me."

This book uncovers the life of the 266th Bishop of Rome, Jorge Mario Bergoglio.

Dear young people, please, don't be observers of life, but get involved. Jesus did not remain an observer, but he immersed himself. Don't be observers, but immerse yourself in the reality of life, as Jesus did.

— Pope Francis, July 27, 2013 Youth Prayer Vigil at Rio

Table of Contents

Introduction 9

Early Life in Argentina 16

Vocation as a Jesuit..22

Dark Days in Argentina..29

Bergoglio's Peaceful Secret Resistance....................35

Growth as a Pastor of Souls 42

A Cardinal for the Poor 49

Promoting a Culture of Cooperation.........................55

A Window to the Soul 63

The Papacy and Resignation of Benedict XVI 72

The Conclave of 2013 80

Pope Francis Greets the World 87

'Bishop and People' 94

Pope Francis and Saint Francis 103

Mercy: A Key to Understanding Pope Francis 110

Church Reform...120

Pope Francis and the Youth 128

Pope Francis' Role in the Church..............................135

The Rosary..141

Introduction

There is something about Pope Francis that captivates and delights people, even people who hardly know anything about him. He was elected in only two days of the conclave, yet many who tried their hand at speculating on who the next pope might be barely included him on their lists. The evening of Wednesday, March 13, 2013, the traditional white smoke poured out from the chimney of the Sistine Chapel and spread throughout the world by way of television, Internet, radio, and social media, signaling the beginning of a new papacy.

As the light of day waned from the Eternal City, some 150,000 people gathered watching intently for any movement behind the curtained door to the loggia of St. Peter's. A little after 8:00 p.m., the doors swung open and Cardinal Tauran emerged to pronounce the traditional and joyous Latin formula to introduce the new Bishop of Rome: "Annuncio vobis gaudium magnum; habemus papam!" ("I announce to you a great joy: we have a pope!") He then announced the new Holy Father's identity: "Cardinalem Bergoglio..."

The name Bergoglio, stirred up confusion among most of the faithful who flooded the square that were even more clueless than the television announcers were, who scrambled to figure out who exactly the new pope was. Pausing briefly, Cardinal Tauran continued by announcing the name of the new pope: "...qui sibi nomen imposuit Franciscum" ("who takes for himself the name Francis"). Whoever this man may be, his name choice resonated with all, and the crowd erupted with jubilant cheers. A few moments passed before the television announcers and their support teams informed their global audiences that the man who was about to walk onto the loggia dressed in white was Cardinal Jorge Mario Bergoglio, age 76, of Buenos Aires, Argentina.

To add to the bewilderment and kindling curiosity, when the new pope stepped out to the thunderous applause of the crowd in St. Peter's Square, he did not give the expected papal gesture of outstretched arms. Instead, he gave only a simple and modest wave. Also, before giving his first apostolic blessing, he bowed asking the faithful, from the least to the greatest, to silently pray for him. These acts were only the beginning of many more words and gestures, such as taking a seat on the bus with the cardinals, refusing a popemobile with bulletproof glass, and paying his own hotel bill after his election, that would raise eyebrows among some familiar with papal customs and delight the masses.

Is he making a pointed critique of previous pontificates? Is he simply posturing a persona to the world at large to make a point? The study of the life of Jorge Mario Bergoglio gives a clear answer, and the answer is no. This is simply who he is as a man and as a priest. The example of his thought-provoking gestures flows from his character, his life experiences, his religious vocation, and his spirituality. This book uncovers the life of the 266th Bishop of Rome, Jorge Mario Bergoglio, also known as Father Jorge, a name he preferred even while he was an archbishop and cardinal.

What exactly do people find so attractive about Pope Francis? Aldo Cagnoli, a layman who developed a friendship with the Pope when he was serving as a cardinal, shares the following: "The greatness of the man, in my humble opinion lies not in building walls or seeking refuge behind his wisdom and office, but rather in dealing with everyone judiciously, respectfully, and with humility, being willing to learn at any moment of life; that is what Father Bergoglio means to me" (as quoted in Ch. 12 of Pope Francis:

Conversations with Jorge Bergoglio, previously published as El Jesuita [The Jesuit]).

At World Youth Day 2013, in Rio de Janeiro, Brazil, three million young people came out to celebrate their faith with Pope Francis. Doug Barry, from EWTN's Life on the Rock, interviewed youth at the event on what features stood out to them about Pope Francis. The young people seemed most touched by his authenticity. One young woman from St. Louis said, "He really knows his audience. He doesn't just say things to say things... And he is really sincere and genuine in all that he does." A friend agreed: "He was looking out into the crowd and it felt like he was looking at each one of us...." A young man from Canada weighed in: "You can actually relate to [him]... for example, last night he was talking about the World Cup and athletes." A young woman added, "I feel he means what he says... he practices what he preaches... he states that he's there for the poor and he actually means it."

The Holy Spirit guided the College of Cardinals in its election of Pope Francis to meet the needs of the Church following the historic resignation of Pope Benedict XVI due to old age. Representing the growth and demographic shift in the Church throughout the world and especially in the Southern

Hemisphere, Pope Francis is the first non-European pope in almost 1,300 years. He is also the first Jesuit pope. Pope Francis comes with a different background and set of experiences. Both as archbishop and as pope, his flock knows him for his humility, ascetic frugality in solidarity with the poor, and closeness. He was born in Buenos Aires to a family of Italian immigrants, earned a diploma in chemistry, and followed a priestly vocation in the Jesuit order after an experience of God's mercy while receiving the sacrament of Reconciliation. Even though he is known for his smile and humor, the world also recognizes Pope Francis as a stern figure that stands against the evils of the world and challenges powerful government officials, when necessary.

The Church he leads is one that has been burdened in the West by the aftermath of sex abuse scandals and increased secularism. It is also a Church that is experiencing shifting in numbers out of the West and is being challenged with religious persecution in the Middle East, Asia, and Africa. The Vatican that Pope Francis has inherited is plagued by cronyism and scandal. This Holy Father knows, however, that his job is not merely about numbers, politics, or even success. He steers clear of pessimism knowing that he is the head of Christ's Body on earth and works with Christ's grace. This is the man God has chosen in these times to lead his flock.

Early Life in Argentina

Jorge Mario Bergoglio was born on December 17, 1936, in the Flores district of Buenos Aires. The district was a countryside locale outside the main city during the nineteenth century and many rich people in its early days called this place home. By the time Jorge was born, Flores was incorporated into the city of Buenos Aires and became a middle class neighborhood. Flores is also the home of the beautiful Romantic-styled Basilica of San José de Flores, built in 1831, with its dome over the altar, spire over the entrance, and columns at its facade. It was the Bergoglios' parish church and had much significance in Jorge's life.

Jorge's father's family had arrived in Argentina in 1929, immigrating from Piedimonte in northern Italy. They were not the only ones immigrating to the country. In the late nineteenth century, Argentina became industrialized and the government promoted immigration from Europe. During that time, the land prospered and Buenos Aires earned the moniker "Paris of the South." In the late nineteenth and early twentieth centuries waves of immigrants from Italy, Spain, and other European countries came off ships in the port of Buenos Aires. Three of Jorge's great uncles were the first in the family to immigrate to Argentina in 1922 searching for better employment opportunities after World War I. They established a paving company in Buenos Aires and built a four-story building for their company with the city's first elevator. Jorge's father and paternal grandparents followed the brothers in order to keep the family together and to escape Mussolini's fascist regime in Italy. Jorge's father and grandfather also helped with the business for a time. His father, Mario, who had been an accountant for a rail company in Italy, provided similar services for the family business (Cardinal Bergoglio recalls more on the story of his family's immigration and his early life in Ch. 1 of Conversations with Jorge Bergoglio).

Providentially, the Bergoglios were long delayed in liquidating their assets in Italy; this forced them to miss the ship they planned to sail on, the doomed Pricipessa Mafalda, which sank off the northern coast of Brazil before reaching Buenos Aires. The family took the Giulio Cesare instead and arrived safely in Argentina with Jorge's Grandma Rosa. Grandma Rosa wore a fur coat stuffed with the money the family brought with them from Italy. Economic hard times eventually hit Argentina in 1932 and the family's paving business went under, but the Bergoglio brothers began anew.

Jorge's father, Mario, met his mother Regina at Mass in 1934. Regina was born in Argentina, but her parents were also Italian immigrants. Mario and Regina married the following year after meeting. Jorge, the eldest of their five children, was born in 1936. Jorge fondly recalls his mother gathering the children around the radio on Sunday afternoons to listen to opera and explain the story. A true porteño, as the inhabitants of the port city of Buenos Aires are called, Jorge liked to play soccer, listen to Latin music, and dance the tango. Jorge's paternal grandparents lived around the corner from his home. He greatly admired his Grandma Rosa, and keeps her written prayer for her grandchildren with him until this day. Jorge recalls that while his grandparents kept their personal conversations in Piedmontese, Mario chose mostly to speak Spanish, preferring to look forward rather than back. Still, Jorge grew up speaking both Italian and Spanish.

Upon entering secondary school at the age of thirteen, his father insisted that Jorge begin work even though the family, in their modest lifestyle, was not particularly in need of extra income. Mario Bergoglio wanted to teach the boy the value of work and found several jobs for him during his adolescent years. Jorge worked in a hosiery factory for several years as a cleaner and at a desk. When he entered technical school to study food chemistry, Jorge found a job working in a laboratory. He worked under a woman who always challenged him to do his work thoroughly. He remembers her, though, with both fondness and sorrow. Years later, she was kidnapped and murdered along with members of her family because of her political views during the Dirty War, a conflict in the 1970's and 80's between the military dictatorship and guerrilla fighters in which thousands of Argentineans disappeared.

Initially unhappy with his father's decision to make him work, Jorge recalls later in his life that work was a valuable formative experience for him that taught him responsibility, realism, and how the world operated. He learned that a person's self worth often comes from their work, which led him to become committed later in life to promote a just culture of work rather than simply encouraging charity or entitlement. He believes that people need meaningful work in order to thrive. During his boyhood through his priestly ministry, he experienced the gulf in Argentina between the poor and the well off, which left the poor having few opportunities for gainful employment.

At the age of twenty-one, Jorge became dangerously ill. He was diagnosed with severe pneumonia and cysts. Part of his upper right lung was removed, and each day Jorge endured the pain and discomfort of saline fluid pumped through his chest to clear his system. Jorge remembers that the only person that was able to comfort him during this time was a religious sister who had catechized him from childhood, Sister Dolores. She exposed him to the true meaning of suffering with this simple statement: "You are imitating Christ." This stuck with him, and his sufferings during that time served as a crucible for his character, teaching him how to distinguish what is important in life from what is not. He was being prepared for what God was calling him to do in life, his vocation.

Vocation as a Jesuit

Before meeting up with his friends at the train station to go and celebrate Student Day on September 21, 1954, Jorge decided to pay a visit to his parish, San José de Flores. Student Day marks the start of spring in the Southern Hemisphere. At church, Jorge was moved and inspired by a priest visiting that day and decided to ask the priest to hear his confession. The overwhelming experience of God's mercy in receiving the sacrament awakened him to his vocation, that God was calling him to the priesthood in the religious life. "Something strange happened to me in that confession. I don't know what it was, but it changed my life. I think it surprised me, caught me with the guard down," Jorge recalls in Ch. 4 of Conversations with Jorge Bergoglio. In that moment, at the age of seventeen, he knew his vocation and was so moved that he stayed in the church praying instead of meeting his friends at the train station to celebrate Student Day.

His experience of God's calling, through the mercy of Confession, became the inspiration for the motto he chose for himself when he was first appointed auxiliary bishop of Buenos Aires and has remained the same during his papacy: "miserando atque eligendo". These Latin words are taken from a homily on Saint Matthew by the Venerable Bede and are translated as "seeing through the eyes of mercy, he chose him" (as translated in Ch. 4 of John Allen's Ten Things Pope Francis Wants You to Know). The complete sentence from the Venerable Bede reads like this: "Jesus, therefore, saw the publican, and because he saw by having mercy and by choosing, He said to him, 'Follow me'" (as translated by Father Zuhlsdorf on 'Father Z's Blog'). The story of Saint Matthew reveals that he had one of the most hated and least ethical professions of his day in 1st century Palestine; he was a tax collector for the Roman occupiers. Yet, Christ showed him merciful love, called him, changed his life, and made him an Apostle.

In a 2013 interview with Father Antonio Spadaro, Pope Francis refers to Caravaggio's painting the Calling of Saint Matthew at the Church of St. Louis in Rome, "It is the gesture of Matthew that strikes me: he holds on to his money as if to say, 'No, not me! No, this money is mine.' Here, this is me, a sinner on whom the Lord has turned his gaze" (as translated in America magazine).

Four years would pass before Jorge tells anyone about his vocational discernment. Meanwhile, he continued his studies and work in food chemistry, but he spent more time alone in silent prayer. He eventually graduated from the University of Buenos Aires. At the age of twenty-one, Jorge felt the time was right to make a serious move toward realizing his vocation. Jorge first told his father about his decision to enter seminary. His father was pleased with his choice, but his mother had a different reaction. When he told his mother, she was hesitant and did not accept his decision for many years. His mother never visited him in seminary, even though they were together when he came home on vacation. Jorge, however, recalls his mother kneeling and asking for his blessing on his ordination day. Jorge kept close to his heart the way his Grandma Rosa was unconditionally supportive of him during his discernment. She was pleased that he was pursuing the priesthood, but also said she would support and welcome him back if he decided it wasn't for him.

Jorge knew that he wanted to join a religious order rather than become a diocesan priest, and he ultimately decided upon the Jesuits, the Society of Jesus. The Society of Jesus, sometimes nicknamed the 'Marines of God,' was founded by St. Ignatius of Loyola in 1534 in Paris and has been at the front lines of evangelization. The Jesuits began their ministry in the land that became known as Argentina in 1586, continuing for centuries to found missions, colleges, schools, parishes, and serving the poor throughout the region. Pope Francis recalls in his 2013 interview with Father Spadaro, S.J., "Three things in particular struck me about the Society: the missionary spirit, community and discipline. And this is strange, because I am a really, really undisciplined person. But their discipline, the way they manage their time—these things struck me so much." He continues, "And then a thing that is really important for me: community. I was always looking for a community. I did not see myself as a priest on my own. I need a community."

Jorge's ordination was subject to a process of discernment, and interest in the opposite sex played its role as well. Before his more serious commitment to the priesthood, he had a crush on a girl his age when he was twelve years old. He said he wanted to marry her, but her parents disapproved. When he was in seminary, Jorge met a very beautiful girl at his uncle's wedding and spent a week struggling on which way he would go. In fact, he recalls that he could not pray that whole week because of his struggle. Still, he remained in seminary and ultimately discerned together with his superiors that his calling to the priesthood was genuine.

The Jesuits have a long and disciplined formation process involving prayer, study, and ministry. For his first three years, Jorge was sent to the archdiocesan seminary, Inmaculada Concepción, in Buenos Aires. After entering the novitiate in 1958, he was sent to Santiago, Chile, to pursue studies in the humanities. In 1960, he took his first vows in the Society of Jesus. In that same year, he earned a licentiate in philosophy, an advanced degree granted by the Church, from the Colegio Máximo San José in San Miguel, Buenos Aires Province, Argentina.

In 1964, Jorge taught literature and psychology at the Colegio de la Inmaculada, a Jesuit secondary school in Santa Fe, Argentina. Two years later, in 1966, he taught at the Colegio del Salvador secondary school in Buenos Aires. He liked being a teacher and loved his students. Jorge reflects in Ch. 5 of Conversations with Jorge Bergoglio, "I love them very much. They never were, nor are they now, indifferent to me, and I never forgot them. I want to thank them for all the good they did me, particularly for the way they taught me how to be more a brother than a father." In one of his literature classes, he had the students try their hand at writing short stories. The students loved the project and the stories were good enough that he was able to have them published together in a book. Jorge's approach to teaching was similar to his approach to everything else; he added a personal touch. He shares, "If you try to educate using only theoretical principles, without remembering that the most important thing is the person in front of you, then you fall into a kind of fundamentalism... they can't absorb lessons that aren't accompanied by a life's testimony and a degree of closeness...." During his days as a teacher, Jorge also taught classes in theology, philosophy, and the humanities.

Jorge Bergoglio, was finally ordained as a priest on December 13, 1969, by Archbishop Ramón José Castellano. In 1972, he became a novice master. Following his tertianship period of formation in Alcalá, Spain, he took his final vows in the Society of Jesus on April 22, 1973. Almost immediately after, he was elected provincial of the order in Argentina and Uruguay, in July 31, 1973, serving until 1979. His tenure as provincial coincided with the Dirty War in Argentina between the military dictatorship and guerrilla fighters. Both groups murdered thousands of their perceived opponents. Meanwhile, a growing number of Jesuits wanted to get involved in the conflict. To say the least, Jorge Bergoglio's job would not be easy.

Dark Days in Argentina

In the early twentieth century, Argentina attracted waves of immigrants as a land of opportunity. The country took a turn in the 1930's and was hit hard by the world financial collapse and a series of economic hardships. The socioeconomic gap between the rich and poor as well as the plague of rising inflation became perennial issues. Politicians with radical ideologies often appealed to the voters in hopes for better days. Military leaders would intervene to topple radical leaders, bringing about juntas and dictatorships that then provoked guerrilla movements to try to overthrow dictators. The country also had the challenge of walking a fine line between the capitalist United States of America and the communist Soviet Union during the Cold War, trying not to anger either superpower.

Juan Perón, a military officer turned populist leader, was elected president in 1946 and brought progress on some fronts while also creating many enemies. He vastly expanded social programs for the poor while brutally silencing his opponents and committing human rights violations. His left-wing ideology was hard to pin down and simply became known as 'Peronism.' He was ousted by the military and exiled in 1955, settling in Spain. Eighteen years later, in 1973, the situation in Argentina had deteriorated such that Perón returned to be elected to a second term at the age of 77. He died the next year and was succeed by his wife, Isabel Martínez de Perón in 1974. By the middle of her short presidency, the Dirty War was underway as she battled anti-communist paramilitary fighters, often continuing her husband's underhanded means to remain in power. She was promptly ousted and exiled by the military in 1976 in the midst of a crisis that saw rocketing inflation in the country.

Intent on rooting out Peronists and communist sympathizers, the military established the 'National Reorganization Process,' which turned out to be a brutal junta lasting several long years, from 1976 to 1983. Under 'Operation Condor,' tens of thousands of Argentines suspected of being political dissidents were kidnapped, tortured, and often killed by the military. Pregnant women who were kidnapped were allowed to give birth and their babies were stolen and given to the families of military officers. Afterwards, the women were killed. Suspected dissidents were thrown from military planes to drown in the Atlantic. Bodies of persons executed on land were often mutilated. Meanwhile, various groups of Marxist guerrilla fighters, including the Montonaros, bombed and assassinated people throughout the country. Thousands were killed and kidnapped. To this day, the Argentine people are still coping with the loss and displacement of people during the Dirty War.

To make matters worse, in 1982, in an attempt to rally nationalism around their regime and distract people from internal problems, the junta invaded the Falkland Islands about a thousand miles off the Argentine coast, a group of islands which has been long claimed by Argentina though ruled by the United Kingdom since 1833. In response, British naval fleets, aircraft carriers, and bombers quickly made their way to the south Atlantic, bringing about a swift victory for the United Kingdom. The Falklands War was over in a little over two months, but it came at the expense of hundreds of casualties and the sinking of several warships on both sides. The loss for Argentina, however, led to the disgrace and ultimate collapse of the junta in 1983 and the restoration of democracy.

Moved by the plight of the poor and the harshness of the government, many Jesuit priests rallied around various liberation theologies that were often mixed with Marxist politics and sometimes involvement with the guerrilla warriors. Father Bergoglio was also very interested in the plight of the less fortunate, but he saw dangers for the Church in many of the strains of liberation theology circulating through Latin America. In secondary school, Father Bergoglio had a communist teacher whom he highly regarded and he even read a communist publication, but he never became a communist. Many in Latin America blamed American capitalism for the economic situation in their countries.

As a priest and provincial, Father Bergoglio realized that the Gospel of Christ could not be reduced to any worldly ideology, especially one that is furthered by violent revolution. Many of these liberation theologies substituted the ultimate Christian hope of heaven with a worldly utopia, crowding out the Gospel's emphasis on liberation from sin and death in favor of liberation from socioeconomic oppression. Furthermore, it was clear to Father Bergoglio that priests, as leaders of the Church and men set apart, must never take up arms or participate in murderous acts against the oppressors. He also had to maintain the safety of the Jesuits during the junta. As provincial, Father Bergoglio was firm with priests who confused preaching the Gospel with furthering ideology and associated closely with the guerrillas. He even had to dismiss some priests from the Society of Jesus who refused to comply.

In the mid 1980's, the Vatican's Congregation for the Doctrine of the Faith issued two corrective documents with regard to liberation theology. The documents, promulgated by then-Cardinal Ratzinger, the future Pope Benedict XVI, affirmed the authentic message of Christian liberation from sin as well as the Church's preferential option for the poor while warning strongly against confusing the Gospel with worldly ideology or violent revolution. After Father Bergoglio became pope, Father Lombardi, the Vatican press secretary, said, "Regarding 'liberation theology': Bergoglio has always referred to the Instructions of the Congregation for the Doctrine of the Faith. He has always rejected violence, saying that its price is always paid by the weakest" (as quoted in Ch. 7 of Pope Francis by Matthew Bunson, which also further explains the situation in Argentina and the Jesuits during that time). Some of the priests' close ties with the resistance, in fact, would lead to near tragedy.

Bergoglio's Peaceful Secret Resistance

Two Jesuits in particular, Father Orlando Yorio and Father Francisco Jalics, who worked among the poor in the favela, or slum, of Buenos Aires persisted in politically charged teachings. Their preaching came to the attention of the junta after the military arrested a man who worked with the priests before joining the guerillas. The two Jesuits disappeared in 1976 and were held captive by the military at the Navy Mechanics School, a site infamous for the torture and killing during the junta.

At the time, the Church in Argentina was often silent about the atrocities of the Dirty War. The bishops later issued apologies for the omissions made by clergy. In the 2000's, victims' advocacy groups accused Cardinal Bergoglio of also being silent about the kidnapping and even, perhaps, abetting the junta with the task. These accusations resurfaced in the media once again when Bergoglio ascended to the papacy.

In 2013, reporter Nello Scavo published a book in Italy, "La Lista di Bergoglio" (Bergoglio's List). He used interviews with former Argentine fugitives, various interviews with Bergoglio, and court documents to reveal what actually took place during the Dirty War. Sandro Magister, a Vatican expert, writes in a review of the book, "What the young provincial of the Argentine Jesuits at the time did during those years long remained a mystery. So dense as to prompt the suspicion that he had passively witnessed the horror, or worse, had exposed to greater danger some of his confrères, those most committed among the resistance." In November 2010, lawyers representing victims of the Dirty War extensively examined Cardinal Bergoglio in a court proceeding and questioned why he met with Jorge Videla and Emilio Massera, leaders of the juanta. Perhaps, they insinuated, he was a co-conspirator with the dictators. After all, during their time in captivity, Father Yorio and Father Jalics were told by their captors that Father Bergoglio was the one that betrayed them, and Father Bergoglio did not publicly call out for their release.

Father Bergoglio recognized that a public call for the release of the priests would be a very dangerous act for both him and his order. Instead, he arranged secretly to plead for their release. In a letter to Father Jalics' brother, Father Bergoglio wrote, "I have lobbied the government many times for your brother's release. So far we have had no success. But I have not lost hope that your brother will soon be released. I have made this affair MY thing. The difficulties that your brother and I have had over the religious life have nothing to do with it" (as quoted in Ch. 7 of Pope Francis by Matthew Bunson).

Risking his own life, Father Bergoglio was determined to speak face to face with Jorge Videla, the general at the helms of the junta government, and Admiral Massera. His interest with Massera, a naval admiral high in the juanta, was to get to Videla in order to plead for the release of the priests. Not successful in his first meeting with Videla, Father Bergoglio committed to try again. Father Bergoglio found the priest who routinely said Mass for Videla at his home and convinced him to call in sick one day so he could trade places with the priest. He went to the general's home to say Mass and then approached Videla. Videla confirmed that, as Father Bergoglio had suspected, Father Yorio and Father Jalics were indeed being held at the Naval Mechanics School. He then approached Massera. In 2010, Bergoglio shared with the court his conversation with the admiral: "'Look, Massera, I want them back alive.' I got up and left." The next day, the two priests were released, after five months into their ordeal, drugged, and dropped from a helicopter into a marsh.

The priests later realized that Father Bergoglio had not betrayed them to the juanta and were reconciled to him. Father Jalics now lives in Germany and has supported Bergoglio's papacy. Father Lombardi at the Vatican countered the attacks on Bergoglio for these events: "The accusations pertain to a use of historical-sociological analysis of the dictatorship period made years ago by left-wing anticlerical elements to attack the Church. They must be firmly rejected" (as quoted in Ch. 7 of Pope Francis by Matthew Bunson). But this was not all. Father Bergoglio in fact had much to hide from the juanta.

Bergoglio admitted in interviews that he helped to hide wanted persons from the juanta during the Dirty War and even provided his own identification to a wanted man who resembled him. The book, "Bergoglio's List", reveals that Father Bergoglio was actually the mastermind of a secret network carefully orchestrated to hide and transport targeted persons. The network worked from a Jesuit institution that was located only a few blocks away from the president's palace. Fugitives were enrolled at the Colegio Máximo seminary in San Miguel as students or retreatants. Neither the fugitives nor Bergoglio's collaborators knew who among them was a fugitive and who was an actual student. They were only told enough information to accomplish their particular mission. According to Magister, "Bergoglio was the only one who held all the strings." Fugitives were often transported to Brazil secretly by land or to Uruguay by cargo boat and passed for hired help. According to Father Juan Scannone, a Jesuit who worked with Father Bergoglio, "If one of us had known and had been abducted and subjected to torture, the whole network of protection would have fallen apart. Father Bergoglio was aware of this risk, and for this reason he kept everything secret. A secret that he maintained even afterward, because he never wanted to boast about that exceptional mission of his."

In addition to saving at least dozens of lives, this time prepared Father Bergoglio for his future leadership in the Church. Father Bergoglio believed that many of his homeland's problems could be boiled down to a lack of solidarity and a lack of concern for one's fellow countrymen that are different either politically or socioeconomically. There were many factions in the country that divide the rich and the poor, and throughout the years many sad and emotionally charged events that have widened that chasm. Even though the country is rich in natural resources, many of the resources have not been developed, which make the cities the main venue for possible employment. The poor lack education and have fallen into a pattern of dependency; many have not had the opportunity to develop a real work ethic. Furthermore, the poverty rate in Argentina has multiplied exponentially over the past decades. Father Bergoglio speaks of the poor, "It is everyone's responsibility: it is mine, just as it is the bishops', all Christians', and those who spend money without a clear social conscience" (see Ch. 10 of Conversations with Jorge Bergoglio for his reflections on the problems within Argentina). Soon enough, Father Bergoglio would have an opportunity on a national scale to do what he could to promote a 'culture of cooperation.'

Growth as a Pastor of Souls

After his term as provincial ended in 1979, Father Bergoglio was assigned as rector of a seminary, wrote several books, pursued advanced studies, and became a leading spiritual director in Ignatian Spirituality. Bergoglio was appointed rector of the Faculty of Philosophy and Theology at the Colegio Máximo San José in San Miguel, an institution where he once studied at and where he had served as a novice director and teacher. He also taught classes in theology while attending to his administrative duties. He wrote and published several books, including Meditaciones para religiosos (Meditations for Religious) in 1982, Reflexiones sobre la vida apostólica (Reflections on the Apostolic Life) in 1986, and Reflexiones de esperanza (Reflections of Hope) in 1992.

Interested in studying the work of Vatican II-era theologian Romano Guardini, the founder of the Communion and Liberation movement, Father Bergoglio received permission to go to Germany in 1986 to consult with professors about a doctoral dissertation. While in Germany, he received further training in spirituality, became fluent in German, and came upon the image of Mary Untier of Knots in Augsburg. He later introduced the image of Mary Untier of Knots in

Argentina for intercession for marital difficulties and other difficult situations in life.

Afterwards, Father Bergoglio was sent to Córdoba in central Argentina to serve as a parish priest and spiritual director. Among Jesuits, he became well known for his expertise in the Spiritual Exercises of St. Ignatius of Loyola, their founder. The Spiritual Exercises involve a prolonged period of reflection, typically 30 days under the guidance of a spiritual director, to meditate and to listen to the voice of God. This time helps one discern which elements in one's life are drawing him closer to God or further away. Father Spadaro, in an interview with Pope Francis, asked what it means for a Jesuit to be elected pope and how it would make a difference in his ministry. The Holy Father's answer was, "Discernment." He continued, "Discernment is always done in the presence of the Lord, looking at the signs, listening to the things that happen, the feeling of the people, especially the poor.... Discernment in the Lord guides me in my way of governing."

Archbishop Ubaldo Calabresi, the papal nuncio to Argentina, and Father Bergoglio became good friends. Calabresi would consult with Bergoglio about priests who were being considered for the episcopacy. One day, the nuncio told Father Bergoglio that he had to meet in person. Father Bergoglio happened to be traveling on a three-stop flight within Argentina, so Calabresi offered to meet at the airport in Córdoba. Father Bergoglio recalls, "It was May 13, 1992. He asked me a range of questions on serious matters. And when the plane...was boarding, he told me, 'Ah... one last thing... you've been named auxiliary bishop of Buenos Aires, and the appointment will be made official on the twentieth.' He came out with it just like that" (from Ch. 12 of Conversations with Jorge Bergoglio). Jesuits are not allowed to seek offices within the Church, although they may accept if under obedience to the pope, to whom Jesuits take a special vow of obedience.

Pope John Paul II made the appointment at the advice of Cardinal Antonio Quarracino, the archbishop of Buenos Aires, because of Bergoglio's intelligence and reputation as a wise spiritual director. Bergoglio was consecrated a bishop on June 27, 1992, and made titular bishop of Auca. He took for his motto the same he would use as pope: miserando atque eligendo (seeing through the eyes of mercy, he chose him).

Bishop Bergoglio's first assignment as auxiliary bishop was as pastoral vicar to his home district of Flores in Buenos Aires. He was responsible for pastoral oversight of the area. The following year, in 1993, he was appointed vicar general of the archdiocese. In this role he was responsible under the cardinal for its daily administration. Scripture tells us, "My son, conduct your affairs with humility, and you will be loved more than a giver of gifts. Humble yourself the more, the greater you are, and you will find mercy in the sight of God" (Sirach 3:17-18). Bishop Bergoglio kept the lowest profile of the auxiliary bishops in the archdiocese and he was often seen engaged in humble pastoral work among young people and the poorest of the poor. He was often found serving in the slums of the city. He appealed to many groups of people, including University students in Flores that sought him out for advice, confession, and spiritual direction.

Several years later, Cardinal Quarracino's health declined such that he asked Rome for a coadjutor archbishop to be appointed to succeed him after his time. Bergoglio recalls, "on May 27, 1997, Calabresi called and asked me to lunch with him. We were drinking coffee, and I was all set to thank him for the meal and take my leave when I noticed that a cake and a bottle of champagne had been brought in. I thought it must be his birthday, and I was just about to offer my best wishes. But the surprise came when I asked him about it. 'No, it's not my birthday,' he replied, grinning broadly. 'It so happens that you are the new coadjutor bishop of Buenos Aires'" (from Ch. 12 of Conversations with Jorge Bergoglio). To the surprise of many, Cardinal Quarracino had recommended Bergoglio as his successor. Realizing he was destined to become the spiritual head of 2.5 million souls, Archbishop Bergoglio continued to humble himself, taking public transportation and often getting around by bicycle.

Bergoglio's first major event as coadjutor archbishop was the Special Assembly for America of the Synod of Bishops in Rome in November 1997. The document "Encounter with the Living Jesus Christ: The Way to Conversion, Communion and Solidarity in America" was produced at the event. It was Archbishop Bergoglio's first experience of the Vatican from the inside and it increased his appreciation of the universal Church. Within several months, on February 28, 1998, Cardinal Quarracino died and Archbishop Bergoglio assumed full jurisdiction of the Archdiocese of Buenos Aires.

Having Father Jorge as archbishop would be an experience indeed for the faithful of Buenos Aires.

A Cardinal for the Poor

Archbishop Bergoglio refused the episcopal palace, taking residence in a small upper apartment in a diocesan building next door to the cathedral. He also refused the grand office reserved for the archbishop, fearing it would be too imposing and far-removed for visitors. He used that office for storage, taking a smaller and more welcoming one instead. Archbishop Bergoglio also refused to hire a cook, choosing instead to cook his own meals as his mother had taught him so many years ago. He also prepared meals for his guests and joked about his cooking, "Well, no one ever died..." (from Ch. 1 of Conversations with Jorge Bergoglio). Average porteños were surprised and delighted to come across the new archbishop in the city, dressed like an ordinary priest, striking up casual conversations with people on the bus or subway, and insisting they call him 'Father Jorge.'

Archbishop Bergoglio took his responsibility to his priests seriously. He wanted to remain approachable to them, so he designated one phone line and a one-hour period in the early morning that allowed for any priest to call him directly to talk about anything they needed without ever going through a secretary. He would also remain for long hours at the bedside of priests who were seriously ill or dying. Archbishop Bergoglio, recalling his days as a seminary professor, remained close to the seminarians of the archdiocese, such that certain classes of seminarians in Buenos Aires have even become known as the 'Bergoglio generation.'

Archbishop Bergoglio did not forget the poor, but promoted a perception of the Church as close and near to the marginalized by his words and actions. He continued to go into the homes of the people in the slums and eat simple meals with them. He also personally supported and encouraged other priests to work in the slums, increasing their numbers in the slums greatly. Further, he established a diocesan vicariate, 'Priests for the Favelas,' to organize and support the priests in their ministry. He met periodically to offer support to families who had missing family members because of the kidnappings that took place in the Dirty War; they were known as the 'desaparecidos.' Father Facundo, a priest that was once one of only six priests working in the favelas, said, "Now there are twenty-four of us because he supports us personally and comes to work in the middle of the street with us. He celebrates Masses for the prostitutes in the Plaza Constitutión, visits the AIDS patients, and also keeps in contact with the families of the desaparecidos, always hoping that at least the truth will set us free" (from Ch. 8 of Francis: Pope of a New World by Andrea Tornielli).

The priests in the favelas have changed lives one person at a time. Miriam, who was at one point of her life a very desperate woman, is one of their success stories. Tornielli, shares Miriam's reflection, "I thought there was no more salvation for me. But in the streets I kept meeting the priest, who would tell me, 'God loves you.' Now I work as a catechism teacher and want to become a therapy aide for drug addicts who want to be cured." Archbishop Bergoglio believed that personal contact in the places where people spend their time is a good practice for reaching the inhabitants of the favelas and for touching everyone else. Bergoglio recalls, "I once suggested to the priests that we rent out a garage, and if we find a willing layperson, we send him there to spend time with people, give religious instruction, and even give Communion to the sick or those who are willing. A parish priest told me that if we did that, the believers wouldn't come to Mass anymore. 'Is that so!' I exclaimed. 'Do you mean to say that you have so many coming to Mass at the moment?'" (as quoted in Ch. 7 of Conversations with Jorge Bergoglio).

Pope John Paul II made Bergoglio a cardinal in 2001, a rank that required a greater level of solicitude for the universal

Church from the archbishop of Buenos Aires. Friends and supporters planned to go to Rome to support him in receiving the red beretta, but Bergoglio asked them to spare the expense, stay in Argentina, and donate their travel-money to the poor. Living out the Church's preferential option for the poor, Cardinal Bergoglio gave the best of his time to the marginalized. On Christmas Day, he never failed to cook for the people of the favelas of Buenos Aires, and he celebrated the Mass of the Lord's Supper during Holy Week in 2008 with young drug rehabilitation patients, washing their feet.

Believing very much that the Church needs to be a place of welcome for both saints and sinners, it distressed Cardinal Bergoglio that some priests refused to baptize the babies of unwed mothers. He insisted that the child was not at fault and that the mothers should be shown mercy, congratulated for choosing life, and offered support. He was saddened that these mothers were not welcomed and forced to go from church to church to find a priest who would agree to do the baptism.

Once in 2004, a mother came to him who had seven children from two different men and never had them baptized because it was too expensive to have all the godparents present. Cardinal Bergoglio offered to baptize the children in his chapel after some brief faith instruction and offered to proceed with the baptism with only two godparents who stood in as proxies for the others. Afterwards, he shared sandwiches and soft drinks to celebrate. The mother was not used to being so welcomed in church, and Bergoglio recalls her saying, "'Father, I can't believe it, you make me feel important.' I replied, 'But lady, where do I come in, it's Jesus who makes you important'" (see Ch. 8 of Pope Francis by Matthew Bunson for more on Cardinal Bergoglio's pastoral style).

Promoting a Culture of Cooperation

In 2001, the Argentine economy came to a screeching halt. While the junta had come to an end in 1983, their structures of control left the country in staggering debt. Furthermore, while democratic elections were restored, demagogues often swayed the voters, making promises impossible to keep and often causing much damage. When world markets plunged in 2001, Argentina was unable to pay its debts and the economy was devastated. Inflation soared 5000%, unemployment jumped to near 18%, and the poverty rate rocketed to near 50%. Average government employees were given a steep pay cut, while as many as 500,000 of its higher-paid employees were not paid at all. Also, while some tried to salvage their savings by sending their money abroad, the bank accounts in Argentina were soon frozen by the government and only allowed small withdrawals. Argentines took to the streets with increasing vigor to protest government policies and vent their frustrations, and often received harsh treatment from the police. Violence broke out, and several people lost their lives. President De la Rúa was forced to resign amid the protests, but the Argentines did not really trust any of the alternative politicians. One in five ballots in the presidential election was cast as an 'anger ballot', a cast without indicating a choice.

In the midst of the crisis, Cardinal Bergoglio, promoting a culture of cooperation, emerged as one of the few leaders able to unite the nation (see Ch. 8 of Pope Francis by Matthew Bunson for more on Bergoglio's actions during this time). The people saw him as a credible voice that looked out for the poor and the middle class. He denounced police brutality against the protesters and urged the protesters to stop the violence. Once, when seeing a woman outside his residence unjustly beaten during the protest, he contacted a high-ranking officer and told the officer what was going on and asked him to stop it. He cautioned against the unrealistic promises of politicians and also warned about exploitive influences from abroad. Cardinal Bergoglio also denounced any proposed solutions that compromised the poor. He told the people that the real way to effect change is to change oneself. Argentina had become a nation too long divided. The country lacked solidarity and trust, and Cardinal Bergoglio recognized the situation as a spiritual problem in need of a spiritual solution.

In 2003, Néstor Kirchner, a highly charismatic figure, became president after a succession of two other short presidencies during the crisis. Cardinal Bergoglio denounced

Kirchner's economic policies because they exploited the poor. Further, the Kirchner government's official economic numbers were likely manipulated in his favor, failing to do justice to the real situation facing the average Argentine. In response, Cardinal Bergoglio had the archdiocese collect its own statistics on inflation and unemployment in Argentina. Kirchner, in turn, lashed out against the Cardinal, calling him the "leader of the opposition." The president decided to make other plans for the annual commemoration of the May Revolution, a day when the president traditionally attends the Te Deum service with the archbishop at the cathedral.

Kirchner finished his term in 2007, and his wife Christina Fernández de Kirchner was elected president after him. Néstor Kirchner died in 2008, and Cardinal Bergoglio mourned his death. Christina de Kirchner sought to bring social change that had already come to many other countries by introducing abortion and same-sex marriage to Argentina. While abortion is prohibited by the Argentine constitution, Christina de Kirchner, backed by the Supreme Court, broadly expanded the exceptions allowed by law. She was also successful in enacting legislation allowing same-sex marriage. Cardinal Bergoglio, preaching as usual on matters of national importance from his pulpit in the beautiful

Buenos Aires Metropolitan Cathedral, strongly denounced both moves. He insisted that protecting the unborn child in all cases from abortion is necessary to secure an absolute value of human rights. He believed that if one is permitted to kill an unborn child in some cases, then human rights could be taken away in 'special' circumstances as well.

A document overseen by Cardinal Bergoglio at the General Conference of the Latin American and Caribbean Bishops Conferences, states the following about abortion: "If we want to maintain a solid and inviolable basis for human rights, we absolutely must recognize that human life must always be defended from the very moment of conception. Otherwise, the circumstances and conveniences of the powerful will always find excuses for abusing persons." In an interfaith dialogue, recorded in the book "On Heaven and Earth", with his friend Rabbi Abraham Skorka, Cardinal Bergoglio shares more thoughts on abortion: "The moral problem with abortion is of a pre-religious nature because the genetic code of the person is present at the moment of conception. There is already a human being. I separate the issue of abortion from any religious concept.... The right to life is the first human right. Abortion is killing someone who cannot defend himself."

Cardinal Bergoglio also believes that same-sex marriage is a serious step in the wrong direction. Bergoglio told Rabbi Skorka that same-sex marriage is an "'anthropologic regression,' a weakening of the institution that is thousands of years old and that was forged according to nature and anthropology." Cardinal Bergoglio also insisted that same-sex marriage be disallowed since children deserve a male father and a female mother. He preached from the cathedral pulpit, "Let us not be naive: it is not a simple political struggle; it is an intention [which is] destructive of the plan of God. It is not a mere legislative project (this is a mere instrument), but rather a 'move' of the Father of Lies who wishes to confuse and deceive the children of God" (as quoted in Ch. 8 of Pope Francis by Matthew Bunson). To Bergoglio's point, Christina de Kirchner responded with a full-page newspaper ad accusing the Cardinal of staying in the Dark Ages.

Construction on the Buenos Aires Metropolitan Cathedral where Cardinal Bergoglio had presided began in the late 16th century, but many significant structural repairs and renovations through the centuries brought it to its current eclectic, but glorious form. Twelve pillars representing the twelve Apostles form a long and tall portico that supports its ornate neoclassical façade. An 18th century dome rises over the massive main altarpiece. The pulpit stands to the side. Cardinal Bergoglio spoke out from that pulpit against many social evils of the city and nation, such as human trafficking and prostitution. He also preached against serious economic inequalities, which grew after the 2001 financial crisis. Fiery preaching from the pulpit in the Metropolitan Cathedral was the Cardinal's preferred method of communicating the spoken word to his archdiocese and the nation. He accepted very few interviews.

Cardinal Bergoglio grew to both national and international prominence among the bishops. In 2001, he was designated the rector of the 10th Assembly of the Synod of Bishops in Rome because the terrorist attacks of September 11 prevented Cardinal Egan of New York from coming to Rome. This opportunity increased his level of exposure among the cardinals and bishops. Next, Cardinal Bergoglio attended the 2005 papal conclave, which followed the death of Pope John Paul II. Cardinal Ratzinger was then elected and became Pope Benedict XVI, and, while the proceedings of a conclave remain a secret, it is widely believed that Cardinal Bergoglio received the second largest number of votes. He returned to

Rome in October 2005, to participate in the 11th Assembly of the Synod of Bishops.

Then in November 2005, he was elected president of the Argentine bishops' conference, and was re-elected to another term in 2008. Cardinal Bergoglio used his role as president to organize his fellow bishops against Kirchners' policies that violated Catholic social teaching. In 2007, Cardinal Bergoglio oversaw the writing of the document released by the General Conference of the Latin American and Caribbean Bishops Conferences, which provided a united pastoral vision for the region. In this role, he was able to bring about a 'culture of cooperation' among the bishops, a skill he would soon need like never before.

A Window to the Soul

Though Bergoglio does not accept many interviews, he has shared enough to give us a glimpse into his personal life and values. When asked, "How would you introduce yourself to a group of people who have no idea who you are?" Cardinal Bergoglio gave a joyful and humble response, "I am Jorge Bergoglio, priest. I like being a priest" (from Ch. 12 of Conversations with Jorge Bergoglio). When asked by Father Spadaro years later, in light of the world seeking increased understanding of the new Roman Pontiff, "Who is Jorge Mario Bergoglio?" Pope Francis responded, "I am a sinner. This is the most accurate definition. It is not a figure of speech, a literary genre. I am a sinner."

The word 'mercy' encapsulates both his pontificate and his vocation. His favorite painting is the White Crucifixion by 20th century French artist Marc Chagall, a Jew. In the painting, Chagall depicts, in the surrealist style, many disturbing and confusing symbols of atrocities committed against the Jewish people. The focal point, and the only point of solace and peace in the painting, is the face of the crucified Jesus in the center with his eyes closed, wearing a Jewish prayer shawl in place of a loincloth. The image of Jesus is resigned and does not give into torment, while also depicting his mercy on the wrongs around him. It is reminiscent of Pope Francis' Latin motto, miserando atque eligendo. The Pope tells Father Spadaro, "I think the Latin gerund miserando is impossible to translate in both Italian and Spanish. I like to translate it with another gerund that does not exist: misericordiando ['mercy-ing']." Perhaps, we could translate the motto as "'mercy-ing' and choosing."

One of Bergoglio's favorite works of literature is the classic 19th century Italian novel, "I Promessi Sposi", translated as "The Betrothed". Pope Francis tells Father Spadaro, "I have read The Betrothed, by Alessandro Manzoni, three times, and I have it now on my table because I want to read it again. Manzoni gave me so much. When I was a child, my grandmother taught me by heart the beginning of The Betrothed: 'That branch of Lake Como that turns off to the south between two unbroken chains of mountains....'" The novel is set in 17th century Italy in a time when the people were burdened both by draconian oppressors and widespread panic and loss due to the Black Death whose torments neither spared the rich nor poor, the oppressor nor the oppressed. The violent and worldly power of Don Rodrigo, greatly feared by all, is contrasted with the mysterious and spiritual power of the one man who has no fear of him, the humble and saintly Father Christoforo.

Father Christoforo carries no weapon and holds no high office. The Capuchin friar, not afraid of death by powerful men or by a terrible disease, is seen dressed in a humble habit, standing up to fearsome oppressors for the people, and tending to the victims of plague in their moment of death. He is the most powerful man in the novel, and surely an inspiration to Bergoglio.

Pope Francis often speaks of goodness, truth, and beauty, aspects of all things that reflect the Creator, as an experience that unifies believers and non-believers. He told journalists who came out to meet the newly-elected Pope on March 16, 2013, "This is something we have in common, since the Church exists to communicate precisely this: Truth, Goodness, and Beauty 'in person.'" Pope Francis has a great appreciation for musical beauty, something that his mother instilled in him when she would gather the children around the radio on Sunday afternoons. He shared with Father Spadaro some of his musical favorites, "Among musicians I love Mozart, of course. The 'Et incarnatus est' from his Mass in C minor is matchless; it lifts you to God! I love Mozart performed by Clara Haskil. Mozart fulfills me.... And then Bach's Passions. The piece by Bach that I love so much is the 'Erbarme Dich,' the tears of Peter in the 'St. Matthew

Passion.' Sublime." He shared, in fact, that he mostly uses the radio to listen to classical music.

Bergoglio is also very much a porteño, a native of Buenos Aires, in his interests. In fact, he shares in the book, "Conversations with Jorge Bergoglio", that Buenos Aires is his favorite place in the world. He enjoys tango, saying, "It's something that comes from within." Bergoglio enjoys maté, a hot tea popular in Argentina made from the evergreen leaves of the yerba maté. It is prepared and drunk from a calabash gourd with a metal straw, called a bombilla, which has a mouthpiece at one end and a sieve at the other. The gourd is filled with dried, crushed leaves, and hot water is added, making for a distinct herb-like flavor. One well-circulated image of the newly elected Pope Francis was one of him sharing maté with President Christina de Kirschner, who, despite their differences, had come to Rome to congratulate him. He was also known for sharing maté in the homes of the poor in the slums of Buenos Aires. Joining as a boy, Pope Francis also continues to pay dues as a member of the San Lorenzo Soccer Club in Buenos Aires, and was recently presented in Rome by members with one of their red and blue jerseys. Members of the club, who support the professional San Lorenzo de Almagro team, are known as the Cuervos or Crows, named after the black worn by their founder, Father Lorenzo Massa, who started the fútbol club to keep boys active and out of trouble.

When it comes to languages, besides Spanish, Bergoglio knows Italian, Portuguese, German, French, Piedmontese, Genoese, and English. While perfectly comfortable in Italian, he finds English the most difficult because of the pronunciation. His understanding of Piedmontese and Genoese, and hence his facility with Italian, are from hearing his older family members converse in these dialects when he was a boy. His fluency in German comes from his days of study in Germany.

Bergoglio has a devotion to St. Thérèse of Lisieux. The 19th century French saint, who also inspired Mother Teresa, is known for her 'Little Way' of small deeds with great love and for her 'Shower of Roses' as a sign of answered prayer. Pope Francis shares in Ch. 12 in the book "Conversations with Jorge Bergoglio" the following: "Whenever I have a problem, I ask the saint not to resolve it, but to take it in her hands and help me accept it, and, as a sign, I almost always receive a white rose." Bergoglio has had good experiences of sharing devotions among the people, especially in Argentina, because they become engrained in the culture and keep the people close to God.

Bergoglio has a heart for those of other rites and faiths. Known to greatly appreciate the beauty and spirit of the Eastern rite liturgies and prayers in the Catholic Church, he was appointed ordinary of Eastern rite Catholics in Argentina that were lacking an ordinary while also serving as archbishop of Buenos Aires.

Cardinal Bergoglio became good friends with Rabbi Abraham Skorka and they published a book together recording their dialogue on religious topics, titled "On Heaven and Earth". Skorka recalls, "Inter-religious dialogue, which acquired special significance after the Second Vatican Council, usually begins with a stage of 'tea and sympathy' before moving on to the trickier subjects. With Bergoglio, there was no such stage. Our conversation began with an exchange of terrible jokes about each other's favored soccer teams and went immediately to the candor of sincere and respectful dialogue. Each of us expressed to the other his particular vision about the many subjects that shape life. There were no calculations or euphemisms, just clear and direct ideas. One opened his heart to the other, just as the

Midrash [the traditional commentary on Scripture by the rabbis] defines true friendship."

In their dialogue, the two religious leaders would alternate in discussing their views and values on a given subject, such as society, culture, morality, God, and religion. One would agree with much of what has been said and then contribute his values, perspectives, and experiences. Even in instances where Bergoglio, as a Catholic archbishop, likely disagreed with Skorka, he typically held back from critiquing him unless there was a misunderstanding that had to be cleared. This represents the style of the dialogue and of their friendship; this experience also sheds light on Pope Francis' approach to many situations.

For Bergoglio, dialogue is the way to harmony and solidarity by recognizing commonality in others and acknowledging differences respectfully. Genuine dialogue, according to Bergoglio, is what is very much lacking in the political climate in Argentina. He shares in "Conversations with Jorge Bergoglio" that people must recognize "that the other person has much to give me, that I have to be open to that person and listen, without judgment, without thinking that because his ideas are different from mine, or because he is an atheist, he can't offer me anything. That is not so. Everyone has something to offer, and everyone can receive something." Further, according to Bergoglio, "Real growth in mankind's conscience can only be founded on dialogue and love. Dialogue and love mean recognizing the differences of others, accepting diversity. Only then can we call it a true community: by not attempting to subject others to my criteria and priorities, by not 'absorbing' others, but by recognizing them as valuable for what they are...."

Bergoglio's approach to dialogue is not grounded in relativism; he is a firm believer in truth with an open heart to love those who may be different. Likewise, Bergoglio's openness to all and his emphasis on commonality do not come from a naiveté of the world's problems or of the Church. Instead, his approach is one of mercy, a type of mercy that presupposes the existence of sin and division among us. As a Church leader, his approach has been like the father in the parable of the prodigal son, standing in the road with open arms, welcoming home his son without any questions.

The Papacy and Resignation of Benedict XVI

On April 2, 2005, at the age of 84, a weary and infirm Pope John Paul II went to his eternal reward after a very full 26-year pontificate. Slated now by Pope Francis to be declared a saint on Divine Mercy Sunday of 2014, the man sometimes called 'John Paul the Great' was known for his prolific papal writings, the profundity of his teachings, attracting large crowds on his trips around the world, his closeness with the youth, and his many canonizations of saints. In the conclave that followed, while the cardinals are sworn to secrecy about the proceedings, it is generally believed that Cardinal Bergoglio received the second largest number of votes. Cardinal Bergoglio was very different in style and emphasis from Pope John Paul II, and his election at that time may have indicated a shift away from him. Vatican expert Vittorio Messori makes an educated speculation based on comments from cardinals that, for this reason, both Cardinal Bergoglio and the other cardinals decided upon Cardinal Ratzinger, a close advisor of Pope John Paul II and his prefect of the Congregation for the Doctrine of the Faith (as recalled in the introduction to Conversations with Jorge Bergoglio).

Cardinal Ratzinger, who was already recognized as one of the greatest theologians of the 20th century, became Pope Benedict XVI at the age of 78. He emerged from the loggia of

St. Peter's on April 19, 2005, with arms outstretched in the style of his predecessor, greeting the crowds with these words: "Dear Brothers and Sisters: After the great Pope John Paul II, the Lord Cardinals have elected me, a simple and humble worker in the vineyard of the Lord." A native of Germany, he took the name 'Benedict' with a view to revitalizing the faith and culture of Europe. The name is reminiscent of Pope Benedict XV, who led the Church during the turbulence of World War I, and St. Benedict of Nursia, known as a spiritual father and patron of Europe.

The former prefect of the Congregation for the Doctrine of the Faith had developed a reputation for being a disciplinarian because many errors had to be corrected under his tenure. Pope Benedict XVI, however, emerged as a warm, fatherly, and reconciliatory world religious leader, though still viewed with suspicion by the secular media and some progressive theologians. Pope Benedict XVI had lived and breathed the culture of the Vatican for many years and restored some of the older traditional trappings of the papacy, traditions that emphasized dignity and distinction from modern society. He issued three encyclical letters, simple and foundational in their scope, yet amazingly deep and penetrating. He established a place for the pre-Vatican II liturgy along side the current liturgy so that priests could celebrate at will. He insisted unswervingly in teaching the full doctrine of the faith, instructing the faithful to practice charity in truth.

Pope Benedict XVI's final encyclical, Caritas in Veritate (Charity in Truth), reaffirmed and promoted Catholic social teaching, emphasizing the Church's preferential option for the poor, concern for the environment, and decrying extreme inequalities throughout the world.

Before becoming pope, Cardinal Ratzinger had submitted his resignation as prefect to Pope John Paul II, hoping to spend his retirement in writing and studying. The Holy Father refused to accept his resignation. As the Pope continued his own work, despite his deteriorating physical condition, choosing to be a model of redemptive suffering, the prefect resigned himself to continue in his service as well, at least until the death of Pope John Paul II. Then he was made pope and had to endure many hardships in the years ahead. The sex abuse scandals continued to boil over in the West, and some even accused Pope Benedict of complacency with the issue when he was a bishop.

A quote from the Crusades period from his insightful Regensburg address, which focused primarily on the unity of faith and reason, was taken out of context and broadcast by the media, angering Muslims around the world. Also, some suspected corruption at the Vatican Bank. Corruption was also rampant within the Curia of the Vatican, as highlighted by the 'Vatileaks' scandal in 2012 in which the Pope's butler stole confidential documents of the Vatican City State that revealed misdeeds and cronyism within the Vatican. The documents were leaked to a journalist that later published them in a book. Meanwhile, the Holy Father, who later revealed that he had a pacemaker for his heart condition, was continuing to grow old and felt he lacked the ability to keep up with the obligations of the modern papacy.

In April 2009, Pope Benedict XVI visited the tomb in Aquila, Italy, of hermit and monk Pope St. Celestine V, who resigned the papacy in 1296 after only a few months, after realizing he was suited more for monastic life than the task ahead. St. Celestine had provided the Church legislation for the resignation of a pope prior to his departure. A pope's resignation must be done in complete freedom, deliberately, and in such a way that his resolve is publicly known. However, St. Celestine ended his days as a prisoner of his successor that feared that he might return. He would repeat to himself, referring to a monk's cell, "You wanted a cell, Peter, and a cell you have." In 2010, Pope Benedict XVI revealed to Peter Seewald in his book-length interview, "Light of the World", that he believed that it is sometimes the duty of a pope to resign. He also revealed that he believed that the work he is meant to do as pope has already been accomplished.

Several major newspapers reported that the Pope Emeritus explained that he was given a mystical experience in which God gave him a strong and sustained desire to pursue a life of prayer, renouncing his office. Father Lombardi, the Vatican press secretary, told journalists that it was ultimately during the Holy Father's trip to Cuba in March 2012, that he realized his limitations due to his age and Pope Benedict definitively, but secretly, resolved that he would resign. Soon the Holy Father was transported around St. Peter's on a motorized platform that Pope John Paul II had once used towards his last days.

Pope Benedict called a consistory of cardinals on February 11, 2013, to approve miracles as part of the canonization process of three soon-to-be saints. At the end of the consistory, the frail 85-year-old Pontiff, still seated in his chair, softly delivered an important message in Latin to the cardinals by way of a microphone - his decision to resign his office effective 8 p.m., February 28, 2013. He said, "After having repeatedly examined my conscience before God, I have come to the certainty that my strengths, due to an advanced age, are no longer suited to an adequate exercise of the Petrine ministry.... In today's world, subject to so many rapid changes and shaken by questions of deep relevance for the life of faith, in order to govern the barque of Saint Peter and proclaim the Gospel, both strength of mind and body are necessary, strength which in the last few months, has deteriorated in me to the extent that I have had to recognize my incapacity to adequately fulfill the ministry entrusted to me.... And now, let us entrust the Holy Church to the care of Our Supreme Pastor, Our Lord Jesus Christ" (as translated in Ch. 1 of Pope Francis by Matthew Bunson).

The eyes of the cardinals met each other, expressing surprise and disbelief. A pope had not resigned since Gregory XII in 1415, in order to end the Great Schism. Pope Benedict had succeeded in keeping his decision a secret; he had only informed a handful of men ahead of time. Pope Benedict's last public Mass as Bishop of Rome was held on Ash Wednesday. Then at 4:45 p.m. on February 28, 2013,

Pope Benedict lifted off from the Vatican by helicopter, the sound of the propellers mixing with that of the tolling bells of the basilica and the cheering of supportive crowds as he flew to Castel Gandolfo, the papal summer residence.

Landing in the close-knit town built near the shore of beautiful Lake Albano, he gave his final message and blessing as pope: "Thank you... [for] your friendship that does me so much good.... As of 8:00 p.m. I will no longer be the Supreme Pontiff of the Catholic Church. I will simply be a pilgrim who is beginning the last part of his pilgrimage on earth. But with my heart, my love, my prayer, with all my inner strength, I will work for the common good and the good of the Church and all humanity...." At 8:00 p.m., the doors of the palace at Castel Gandolfo were closed, the papal apartment at the Vatican was sealed, and the Ring of the Fisherman was defaced so the seal could not be used again. The historic papal interregnum had begun.

The Conclave of 2013

'Papabili' is the Italian word for persons who are likely to become pope. Technically speaking, the cardinal-electors of a conclave (those cardinals who are under the age of 80) can elect any baptized Catholic male without impediments as pope, but most popes that are elected are cardinals. In 2013, the 76-year-old Cardinal Bergoglio was near the bottom of the list of papabili, mostly because of his age. Since Pope Benedict had referred to the limitations of his advanced age in his resignation speech, people speculated that the cardinals gathering for conclave would be looking for a younger member of their ranks.

One major concern among the cardinals was finding someone capable of reforming the Church in the face of the sex abuse scandals and to provide solid management for the Roman Curia and the Vatican Bank, which had become a source of scandal. They also desired a man of dynamic faith who was a vibrant communicator and evangelizer capable of reaching out to the modern world, such as the youth, the media, people of various countries and situations, and those who have become alienated from the Church. Other factors they considered included the ability to speak a number of popular languages and a level of comfort with communicating through modern technology. Pope

Benedict's Twitter handle '@Pontifex,' by which he would periodically send out inspirational 'tweets' on matters of faith, had become quite popular in the online world (Matthew Bunson further explains the cardinals' concerns and expectations in Ch. 3 of Pope Francis).

Over the past 500 years, popes have typically come from Italy since most of the cardinals appointed were Italian. The trend in modern times, however, changed with the election of Cardinal Wojtyla of Krakow as Pope John Paul II and then Cardinal Ratzinger of Germany as Pope Benedict XVI. The face of the College of Cardinals has also changed over the past decades to better reflect the universality of the Church, hence increasing the probability of newly elected popes being other than Italian. Italy still has the largest number of cardinals, but is now followed by the United States. Matthew Bunson, in his book, lists the global breakdown of cardinals: 61 from Europe, 17 from North America, 16 from South America, 11 from Africa, 11 from Asia, and 1 from Oceania. Also, while declining in Europe and North America, due to increased secularism, Catholicism is growing considerably in the Southern Hemisphere and Asia, even though the persecution of Christians has become an epidemic in the Middle East, Africa, and Asia. The vocation crisis plaguing

Europe and North America is non-existent in many of these young churches, which now represent the future of the Church. Overall, and thanks to the developing world, the Catholic Church, which literally means 'Universal Church,' is growing, and has about 1.3 billion members worldwide.

Cardinal Angelo Scola of the prominent see of Milan, Italy, an excellent communicator and a top theologian, was among the favored papabili. There was also much talk of Cardinal Peter Turkson of Africa, the president of the Pontifical Council for Justice and Peace. British bookies placed their bets on Cardinal Tarsicio Bertone, the experienced Vatican secretary of state and highest-ranking Vatican official after the pope, despite his involvement with the status quo within the Curia. Cardinal Sean O'Malley of Boston and Cardinal Timothy Dolan of New York were on the top of some lists. However, even the American cardinals noted that regardless of the quality of an American candidate, a pope from the United States might not be ideal in the current world situation, for it may be perceived abroad as another symbol of American world dominance.

The 55-year-old Cardinal Luis Tagle of Manila, a charismatic and youthful figure, was a favorite among some, however his election as pope would likely mean a pontificate even longer than that of Pope John Paul II. Cardinal Marc Ouellet of Canada, prefect of the Congregation for Bishops and known for his selection of excellent candidates for the episcopacy, was also mentioned among the papabili. If one is looking for a Latin American candidate, there was Cardinal Odilo Sherer of São Paulo, Brazil, but as the saying goes, "He who enters the conclave as a 'pope' leaves it as a cardinal."

Pope Benedict had given a motu proprio decree allowing for the College of Cardinals to move the beginning of the conclave forward since the Pope had not died and a funeral was not taking place. However, the cardinals settled upon a relatively later date at the urging of American cardinals who wanted to allow for more time for cardinals to get to know each other. This would give a candidate from outside the Roman Curia a better chance of being elected. The cardinals gathered on March 12, 2013, to concelebrate the Mass for the Election of the Roman Pontiff at St. Peter's Basilica. The last Mass of this type was presided over by Cardinal Ratzinger. This time, Cardinal Angelo Sodano, dean of the College of Cardinals, preached on the most important quality the next pope should have; a heart like Christ the Shepherd.

The cardinals then processed to the Sistine Chapel, with its famous fresco of the Last Judgment as a reminder to them, and chanted Veni Creator Spiritus (Come Creator Spirit), since it is ultimately the Holy Spirit who guides them in selecting the next Roman Pontiff. Then each of the cardinal-electors took an oath in Latin to secrecy and to obey the guidelines laid down for the conclave. Once this was complete, Cardinal Sodano pronounced the traditional words to indicate that all but the cardinal-electors must leave: "extra omnes" ("all others"). Slowly, he walked down the long aisle between the cardinals to seal the doors shut. The only communication the cardinals would have with the outside world was the color of the smoke they would send through the chimney of the Sistine Chapel - black to indicate a vote shy of the two-thirds majority for electing the Roman Pontiff and white to indicate a successful election.

Cardinal Timothy Dolan explains, in a recent ebook "Praying in Rome", what it is like being a cardinal at a papal conclave, "At the start of the conclave, three scrutatori, three cardinals who are in charge of the ballots, were chosen by lot. They would do the counting and make sure that there is always an exact number of ballots. No debating or conversation goes on during the conclave. The actual time we spent in the

Sistine Chapel was an occasion for silence, prayer, and reflection; it is almost a liturgy, a retreat." The papabili do not campaign, and they are not allowed to. The cardinals do have plenty of opportunity to discuss candidates and issues over meals. "Inside the Sistine Chapel, there's immense prayer and deep reflection. But outside of it, when we would leave the Sistine and return for meals and the night to Sanctae Marthae, there were very frank and candid conversations. I would ask brother cardinals, 'What's he like?' or 'Tell me about him. Is the perception accurate?'"

Black smoke poured out of the chimney of the Sistine Chapel four times over two days. A seagull perched on the barren chimney Wednesday afternoon, seemingly waiting with the rest of the world for white smoke. Then, just after 7:00 p.m. of the second day, Wednesday, March 13, white smoke was clearly seen billowing out from the chimney as an ecstatic and growing crowd poured into St. Peter's Square.

Pope Francis Greets the World

The large processional cross rising into view from the balcony signaled to the crowd below the imminent greeting by the new pope, introduced first by Cardinal Tauran as 'Francis.' Jorge Bergoglio, the man who stepped out on the loggia from behind that cross, was not exactly who they had been expecting, and neither were his actions. He was dressed in a simple white cassock and white zucchetto, without the beautiful and elaborate stole and red cape worn by his predecessors at their first address. It almost seemed he didn't know what to do with the sustained cheering that awaited him. He gave one modest wave and then stood motionless as he gazed out stunned onto the lighted St. Peter's Square to the huge crowd that had gathered there after dusk for this very purpose.

He finally addressed the crowds, "Brothers and sisters, good evening! You know that it was the duty of the Conclave to give Rome a Bishop. It seems that my brother Cardinals have gone to the ends of the earth to get one... but here we are... I thank you for your welcome. The diocesan community of Rome now has its Bishop. Thank you!" The new Holy Father's Argentine friends would surely catch the reference to their homeland as the 'End of the World,' stretching over 2,300 miles from the mountainous Bolivian border southward to the Terra del Fuego, separated from Antarctica by the Drake Passage.

The preferred title Pope Francis chose for himself then and thereafter was 'Bishop.' A 'pope,' which means 'father,' is father to the universal Church, and has jurisdiction over the Church because he is the successor of the Apostle Peter. Christ gave the keys of the Kingdom to Peter in Matthew 16:18: "You are Peter [which means Rock], and upon this rock I will build my church...." As Providence would have it, Peter became head of the local church at Rome, the capital of the empire that engulfed the Mediterranean Sea, and the lands that surrounded it: the civilized western world.

There are two reasons that Pope Francis prefers to refer to himself as a bishop. First, wanting always to promote what he calls a "culture of encounter" through closeness to the people, he sees his relationship as bishop of the diocesan community of Rome as modeling the relationship that should take place between the clergy around the world and their congregations. While a pope is a world leader, governing millions of people he cannot meet in person, a bishop gets to know many people in his diocese and the people have the opportunity to get to know the bishop, even often developing a relationship with him. As pope, Francis' relationship with the faithful of Rome is an important example for clergy to be pastors who, as he says, should be "shepherds living with the smell of their sheep" and leaders who foster the spiritual communion and fraternity of the local church.

Pope Francis' words are reminiscent of the words said at Mass, "Remember, Lord, your Church, spread throughout the world, and bring her to the fullness of charity, together with [Francis] our Pope and [N.] our Bishop and all the clergy" (from Eucharistic Prayer II as translated by ICEL). Francis, Bishop of Rome, continues in his first address, "And now, we take up this journey: Bishop and People. This journey of the Church of Rome which presides in charity over all the Churches. A journey of fraternity, of love, of trust among us."

The second reason for preferring to be called a bishop is ecumenical. Pope Francis, as a former ordinary for Eastern rite Catholics in Argentina that were in communion with Rome, also has to connect with those Eastern Christians that were separated from Rome in 1054, a time of the first great division in Christianity. The split happened over a crisis being handled in an uncharitable manner and ended with bishops excommunicating each other. While Catholics and Eastern Christians share a great deal in their beliefs, one difference is the Eastern belief in the collegiality of the bishops in such a way that the Apostle Peter was first among equals.

In contrast, Catholics believe in the primacy of the pope with universal jurisdiction. Vatican II, however, affirmed that the collegiality of bishops and the primacy of the pope are compatible, when properly understood. Father Spadaro recalls in his interview with the Pope, "Pope Francis spoke about 'the path of collegiality' as the road that can lead the church to 'grow in harmony with the service of primacy.' So I ask: 'How can we reconcile in harmony Petrine primacy and collegiality? Which roads are feasible also from an ecumenical perspective?'" The Pope responded, "We must walk together: the people, the bishops and the pope. Synodality [the gathering of bishops to work out Church matters] should be lived at various levels." The Eastern Christians were listening; Bartholomew, Ecumenical Patriarch of Constantinople, chose to attend Pope Francis' inaugural Mass on March 19, 2013, representing the first of his line ever to do so.

Twice during his first address, the Bishop of Rome asked the people to pray. First, he led them in the three most basic and universal prayers memorized by the faithful as children, Our Father, Hail Mary, and Glory Be, for "our Bishop Emeritus, Benedict XVI." Next, he told them, "Let us always pray for one another. Let us pray for the whole world, that there may be a great spirit of fraternity. It is my hope for you that this journey of the Church, which we start today... will be fruitful for the evangelization of this most beautiful city."

Before imparting his first Apostolic blessing, an expectation of all new popes, he bowed and asked the people to pray for him, also emphasizing the role of the laity within the Church in walking together with their pastors. "And now I would like to give the blessing, but first - first I ask a favor of you: before the Bishop blesses his people, I ask you to pray to the Lord that he will bless me: the prayer of the people asking the blessing for their Bishop. Let us make, in silence, this prayer: your prayer over me." Then, after the people's silent prayer, he briefly donned the ornate papal stole while giving the Apostolic blessing before promptly taking it off.

After the blessing, he parted with these words: "Brothers and sisters, I leave you now. Thank you for your welcome.

Pray for me and until we meet again. We will see each other soon. Tomorrow I wish to go and pray to Our Lady, that she may watch over all of Rome. Good night and sleep well!" It would not be long before the people saw the 'Bishop' again.

'Bishop and People'

Cardinal Dolan recalls, in "Praying in Rome", what happened later that evening after the Pope's first address. "After his appearance on the balcony, we were all to return to the Domus Sanctae Marthae for dinner. We piled into one of several buses waiting for us cardinals, while the new Holy Father had a sedan, with proper security escort, ready to chauffeur him back to the Domus. When I got off the bus, my brother cardinals and I waited for the Holy Father to arrive. And when the last bus pulled up, guess who got off? Pope Francis! I guess he told his driver, 'That's OK. I'll just go with the boys, as I have been doing.'" The cardinals would see Pope Francis soon at dinner. Cardinal Dolan recalls, "That night we had, as you might imagine, a rather festive supper. At its conclusion, Cardinal Tarcisio Bertone, the Secretary of State, toasted the new Holy Father. Pope Francis stood to reply. His toast to the cardinals who had just elected him as Successor of St. Peter? 'May God forgive you for what you've done!' which brought the house down."

Pope Francis later retired to Room 207 that night at the Domus Sanctae Marthae, just as he had done during the rest of the conclave. Several days later, he was still living at that room which had been assigned to him during the conclave. Then on March 26, Father Lombardi made the announcement that Room 201 in the Domus would be Pope Francis' new home instead of the large papal apartment. The Holy Father's decision to remain there was the result of Jesuit-inspired discernment and communal living, and his usual theme of closeness to the people.

Pope Francis told Father Spadaro, referring to the communal life of the Jesuits, "I was always looking for a community. I did not see myself as a priest on my own. I need a community. And you can tell this by the fact that I am here in Santa Marta. At the time of the conclave I lived in Room 207. This room where we are now was a guest room. I chose to live here, in Room 201, because when I took possession of the papal apartment, inside myself I distinctly heard a 'no.' The papal apartment in the Apostolic Palace is not luxurious. It is old, tastefully decorated and large, but not luxurious. But in the end it is like an inverted funnel. It is big and spacious, but the entrance is really tight. People can come only in dribs and drabs, and I cannot live without people. I need to live my life with others."

The Domus Sanctae Marthae (St. Martha's House) was built in 1996 by Pope John Paul II to house the cardinals gathering for a conclave to elect the pope. When there is no conclave, the simple modern high-rise complex is used as a guesthouse for those coming on church business to the Vatican. Father Spadaro describes Pope Francis' room that he was invited to for the interview, "The setting is simple, austere. The workspace occupied by the desk is small. I am impressed not only by the simplicity of the furniture, but also by the objects in the room. There are only a few. These include an icon of St. Francis, a statue of Our Lady of Luján, patron saint of Argentina, a crucifix and a statue of St. Joseph sleeping, very similar to the one which I had seen in his office at the Colegio Máximo de San Miguel, where he was rector and also provincial superior."

It is in this room that Pope Francis rises each day at 4:45 a.m. According to Andrea Tornielli, in the Vatican Insider, "The first few hours of Francis' day are dedicated to prayer and meditation on the Readings which the Pope comments on, in the brief homilies he gives in his morning masses in the chapel of the place he likes to call the 'boarding school', commonly known as St. Martha's House: a simple and modern building decorated with light-coloured marble and stained glass. The Bishop of Rome sits in the pews at the back of the chapel to pray. These spontaneous but not completely improvised morning preachings are one of the most important changes of the new pontificate.... The Pope is assisted by cardinals, bishops or visiting priests and the masses are attended mostly by Vatican staff – from IOR staff to rubbish collectors – and their families. Francis greets all of them one by one and then has breakfast in the St. Martha's House 'common room.'"

Prayer is essential for Pope Francis. He said in Ch. 4 of Conversations with Jorge Bergoglio, "In my view, prayer should be an experience of giving way, of surrendering, where our entire being enters the presence of God. It is where a dialogue happens, the listening, the transformation. Look to God, but above all feel looked at by God." The Rosary and Adoration before the Blessed Sacrament remain some of Pope Francis' favorite forms of prayer, besides, of course, celebrating the Mass.

Cardinal Bergoglio was accustomed to wearing old and worn shoes, but just before he went to Rome, friends gave him a pair of new black shoes to make sure he would be suitably dressed for the conclave. Cardinal Bergoglio, after all, was the type that even after being made a cardinal, refused to order new robes, choosing instead to have alterations done on the ones worn by his predecessor. So when he was raised to the papacy, Matthew Bunson tells us in Ch. 8 of Pope Francis, that Pope Francis refused the papal red shoes, preferring the black ones his friends from Argentina had given him. He also refused to wear the jeweled gold cross typically worn by the pope, choosing to keep the metal pectoral cross he had worn as bishop and was designed after the image of Jesus from his favorite painting; White Crucifixion by Marc Chagall. In keeping with his simplicity, he even told his driver on the morning of March 14, to stop by the hotel where he had stayed prior to the conclave so he could personally pay his hotel bill. He also personally made a phone call to Argentina to cancel his Buenos Aires newspaper subscription; he would no longer need it.

Pope Francis' first homily as pope was at the widely anticipated Missa Pro Ecclesia (Mass for the Church) in the Sistene Chapel. While this homily is typically a ponderous one, Pope Francis, keeping mind that the cardinals were not the only ones present and that the flock of the Church throughout the world were also listening, kept his tone and style very simple and pastoral as he would do with all his papal homilies. He focused on a simple theme from the readings, in this case 'movement', which relates to life. It was his practice to number a short list of aspects on that theme, reviewing the points again at the end.

He also refrained from using theological terminology that may not be understood by the people. Instead, he has become known for using his own sayings and freshly coined metaphors. Andrea Tornielli remarks, in "Vatican Insider", on the Pope's morning homilies, "Every morning Francis comes up with new and effective illustrations to his messages, such as the 'babysitter' church, the concept of 'God spray', confession not being like a 'dry cleaner's', 'sitting room Christians', 'museum-piece Christians' and 'starch-pressed Christians'. Then there are his references to 'prayers of courtesy', the 'balm of memory', 'adolescent progressivism' and 'pastoral customs' which instead of fostering people's faith, complicate it. But the most striking thing about Francis is the simplicity of his words. Particularly those about tenderness and forgiveness: 'The message of Jesus is mercy. For me, I say this humbly, it is the Lord's most powerful message.' This message has encouraged people across the world to return to the Church and to confession after years of estrangement."

With Holy Week soon approaching, the new Holy Father made special arrangements for Holy Thursday Mass. While typically the papal Holy Thursday Mass and its rite of foot-washing are held at the Basilica of St. John Lateran, the cathedral of Rome, Pope Francis chose to emphasize the Church's preferential option for the poor by celebrating it instead at the Casal del Marmo youth prison just outside Rome, like he had done previously as a cardinal in Buenos Aires. At his Last Supper, Jesus had washed the feet of his disciples, saying to them, "Do you realize what I have done for you? You call me 'teacher' and 'master,' and rightly so, for indeed I am. If I, therefore, the master and teacher, have washed your feet, you ought to wash one another's feet" (John 13:12-14).

Conveying the message that Jesus and his Church have come to serve all people and especially the poor, Pope Francis washed and kissed the feet of twelve young people who were incarcerated. He did so without distinction of who they were, and chose to also include two young women and two Muslims in the rite of foot-washing. News headlines around the world broadcast the Pope's actions since women and non-Christians had never been included before in a Holy Thursday rite of foot-washing by a pope. Father Lombardi had to explain that the Holy Father is not strictly bound by the liturgical norm that includes only men in the rite. The media had only good things to say about this new pope, forgetting, at least for a bit, their litany of criticisms of the Catholic Church.

Pope Francis and Saint Francis

On March 16, the new Holy Father met with 5,000 journalists in the modern Paul VI Audience Hall at the Vatican. He greeted them warmly, praised their profession, and called on them to communicate goodness, truth, and beauty. It was an important meeting, and he won them over with his charm, humor, and authenticity. He also shared why he choose his name:

"Some people wanted to know why the Bishop of Rome wished to be called Francis. Some thought of Francis Xavier, Francis De Sales, and also Francis of Assisi. I will tell you the story. During the election, I was seated next to the Archbishop Emeritus of São Paolo and Prefect Emeritus of the Congregation for the Clergy, Cardinal Claudio Hummes [OFM]: a good friend, a good friend! When things were looking dangerous [indicating that it would be likely Bergoglio would be elected pope], he encouraged me. And when the votes reached two thirds, there was the usual applause, because the Pope had been elected. And he gave me a hug and a kiss, and said: 'Don't forget the poor!' And those words came to me: the poor, the poor. Then, right away, thinking of the poor, I thought of Francis of Assisi.

"Then I thought of all the wars, as the votes were still being counted, till the end. Francis is also the man of peace. That is how the name came into my heart: Francis of Assisi. For me, he is the man of poverty, the man of peace, the man who loves and protects creation; these days we do not have a very good relationship with creation, do we? He is the man who gives us this spirit of peace, the poor man....How I would like a Church which is poor and for the poor!"

While at first glance it might seem odd for a Jesuit to choose St. Francis as his patron, in considering the life of both Pope Francis and St. Francis, the connection becomes quite clear. St. Francis was born ca. 1181 in Assisi, in the Umbria region in central Italy, to the family of a wealthy silk merchant. As a young man, he enjoyed parties and desired fame and glory. He went off to war but became seriously ill and received a vision in which Christ spoke to him from the crucifix telling him to rebuild his Church. This created a great change in Francis who took the words literally and began rebuilding the chapel in which he prayed that had fallen into ruin. During this time, he also grew closer to the Lord. His father became angry with Francis because Francis had abandoned his route of worldly success and gave away clothes from his father's business to the poor. In turn, Francis gave back all he had to his father, even the clothes off his back.

A sermon on the Gospel further deepened the saint's understanding of his calling and direction. In the Gospel passage, Jesus instructed his disciples who were sent forth to spread the Good News, "Do not take gold or silver or copper for your belts; no sack for the journey, or a second tunic, or sandals, or walking stick" (Matthew 10:9-10). Francis also read this passage literally, which led him to full dependence on God as he went about preaching, choosing 'Lady Poverty' for himself, giving alms to the poor, and begging each day for all his necessities. Francis' authenticity attracted followers to his way of life. Francis petitioned the Pope to grant his blessing to the new religious order, the Friars Minor (lesser brothers), and Pope Innocent III was moved by a dream he had of Francis and agreed.

Once, St. Francis came upon a leper who was begging. At first repulsed by the leper, Francis overcame his fear, embraced the leper, and gave him alms, realizing that love and acceptance is what he needed the most. Some of the stories of the saint and his many miracles reflect his closeness and concern for animals and other creatures as reflections of

God and as brothers and sisters, creatures of the same God. Francis also was determined to take action regarding the bloody Crusades. He met with the Sultan to convert him and win peace, or otherwise face a likely martyrdom. Yet Francis' authenticity won the respect of the Sultan, though he neither became a Christian nor ended the war.

In his later days, Francis, who had conformed his life so closely to that of Christ and whose miracles even echoed those of his Master, was given the grace of the stigmata, the wounds of Christ's crucifixion on his hands and feet. In 1226, St. Francis died, lying naked on the ground since he desired to leave the world in the same manner in which he had come, in utter poverty and dependence on God.

On October 4, 2013, Pope Francis visited the picturesque town of Assisi to celebrate the memorial of St. Francis with a Mass in the courtyard of the beautiful Basilica of St. Francis. There he explained Franciscan peace: "Franciscan peace is not something saccharine. Hardly! That is not the real Saint Francis!" While Franciscan peace is an antidote to violence and unjust war, its domain is within the heart and exudes outward. It is the peace that Francis had in risking his life to embrace the leper and to speak with the Sultan. Pope

Francis continued, "Nor is it a kind of pantheistic harmony with forces of the cosmos... That is not Franciscan either; it is a notion some people have invented!" We are not one with the world, but we are all creatures of the same God. The Pope continued to identify true Franciscan peace: "The peace of Saint Francis is the peace of Christ, and it is found by those who 'take up' their 'yoke', namely, Christ's commandment: Love one another as I have loved you." The love of Christ is a hard command - to love even when it hurts, even in the face of evil. The Holy Father then explained the link of Franciscan peace to humility: "This yoke cannot be borne with arrogance, presumption or pride, but only with meekness and humbleness of heart."

On August 21, 2013, the Syrian regime killed hundreds of civilians in a chemical weapons attack during its ongoing civil war. The photos of the dead soon flooded the Internet and shocked the world. The brutal regime had been at war for some time with rebels that were equally contemptuous of civil rights. By September, the U.S. and its allies were making preparations for an attack on Syria to assist the rebels. Pope Francis spoke out strongly for peace. The Holy Father tweeted on September 2, "War never again! Never again war!" He called on all people of good will to join on

September 7 for a day of prayer and fasting for peace and hosted a televised prayer vigil at the Vatican. In a series of continuous messages on peace, he tweeted on October 7, "The only war we all must fight is the war against evil." Pope Francis strongly denounced the use of chemical weapons, and also denounced unnecessary intervention by outside parties that could make matters worse. He encouraged all parties to dialogue and to look beyond their own interests. Dialogue in Syria was indeed given a chance. As of October 7, both the U.S., the leading voice against the Syrian regime, and Russia, a strategic ally of Syria, expressed cautious optimism over the process of destroying the stockpile of chemical weapons and the regime had agreed. The civil war, however, rages on, and the international situation remains tenuous.

Mercy: A Key to Understanding Pope Francis

Upon selecting a papal coat of arms, Pope Francis retained the shield of his coat of arms from his days as bishop, placing it in front of the traditional symbols of the papacy. Pope Benedict had replaced the triple-layered tiara atop the papal coat of arms with the simpler miter of the Bishop of Rome. The three golden horizontal stripes represented the authority given to Peter stretching to heaven, earth, and under the earth. Two keys of St. Peter are crossed behind it, joined by a red cord. Pope Francis retained these traditional symbols. For the shield of his coat of arms, Pope Francis retained his own former blue shield. Symbols of the Society of Jesus are placed at the center; a golden sun with 32 rays with the monogram IHS in the center capped with a cross and having three nails crisscrossed below it. IHS stands for Iesus Hominem Salvator (Jesus, Savior of Men). Below and on each side, Pope Francis placed his own chosen symbols. To the bottom left is an eight-point golden star, representing the Blessed Mother. In fact, Pope Francis had his pontificate dedicated to Our Lady of Fatima on May 13 before dedicating the whole world to her on October 13. To the right is a golden clump of spikenard flowers, a symbol popular in Latin America for St. Joseph.

During Vatican II, Pope John XXIII had added St. Joseph, chaste husband of the Virgin Mary and patron of the universal Church, to the Roman Canon of the Mass. On May 1, 2013, Pope Francis added St. Joseph to all the other options for the Eucharistic Prayer to ensure that the model of fatherhood, chastity, humility, and service would be included in the prayers of every Mass throughout the world. Pope Francis chose March 19, the feast of St. Joseph, as the date for his inaugural Mass.

Beneath the coat of arms is a scroll that carries his motto, miserando atque eligendo (seeing through the eyes of mercy, he chose him). If there is one word to encapsulate Francis' pontificate, it is 'mercy'. At his first Angelus at St. Peter's Square on March 17, Pope Francis told the crowd, "Never forget this: The Lord never gets tired of forgiving us. It is we, who get tired of asking for forgiveness." Offering God's mercy is Pope Francis' answer to the problems and evils of the world and the people who are entangled in them. Pope John XXIII at his opening speech on October 11, 1962, at the Second Vatican Council - the gathering of the bishops of the world which met from 1962 to 1965, pastorally touching nearly every aspect of the Church's life - exhorted the bishops, "Nowadays... the Spouse of Christ prefers to make use of the medicine of mercy rather than that of severity. She considers that she meets the needs of the present day by demonstrating the validity of her teaching rather than by condemnations."

To the same extent that Franciscan peace is often misunderstood for a shallower counterfeit, mercy is too often subjected to a similar misunderstanding. Mercy is not naiveté of evil that assumes that "I'm okay, you're okay." Mercy should not be confused with moral relativism. Instead, mercy is the voice that tells us to "hate the sin but love the sinner." It understands that sin is something that eats away at the person, but still encourages the person sinning to be treated as a person and with love. It was with mercy that Jesus told the women he saved from those who wished to stone for her adultery, "Go, [and] from now on do not sin any more" (John 8:11).

Pope Francis constantly reminds us in his homilies to have mercy on others by refraining from gossip. In a homily on September 13 at Sanctae Marthae to the Vatican staff, he preached, "The Lord does not waste many words on this concept. Further on [in the Gospel] he says that he who has hatred in his heart for his brother is a murderer." There is no room for gossip in the life of a Christian, and it arises from judging others. Gossip and judgment destroy solidarity and break down the culture of cooperation. Instead of gossiping, Pope Francis urges the people, "Go and pray for him! Go and do penance for her! And then, if it is necessary, speak to that person who may be able to seek remedy for the problem. But don't tell everyone!" Gossip was also a theme of special interest in Bergoglio's homilies as cardinal.

The topic of mercy came up in Pope Francis' interview with Father Spadaro. The Holy Father said, "A person once asked me, in a provocative manner, if I approved of homosexuality. I replied with another question: 'Tell me: when God looks at a gay person, does he endorse the existence of this person with love, or reject and condemn this person?' We must always consider the person. Here we enter into the mystery of the human being. In life, God accompanies persons, and we must accompany them, starting from their situation. It is necessary to accompany them with mercy." Here his answer focuses not on the question of homosexuality, but on mercy. Pope Francis has always said that he follows the teachings of the Catechism of the Catholic Church in all things. The Catechism states in paragraph 2357 that "tradition has always declared that 'homosexual acts are intrinsically disordered.' They are contrary to the natural law. They close the sexual act to the gift of life. They do not proceed from a genuine affective and sexual complementarity. Under no circumstances can they be approved."

The Catechism continues in paragraph 2358 regarding homosexual persons, "This inclination, which is objectively disordered, constitutes for most of them a trial. They must be accepted with respect, compassion, and sensitivity. Every sign of unjust discrimination in their regard should be avoided. These persons are called to fulfill God's will in their lives and, if they are Christians, to unite to the sacrifice of the Lord's Cross the difficulties they may encounter from their condition." What Pope Francis is saying is not new; it is a pastoral application of the teachings of the Catechism with an emphasis on mercy and the person.

Journalists approached Pope Francis on his flight back from World Youth Day in Rio de Janeiro about rumors of gay priests within the Vatican. As usual, his response was a disarming one that looked to the person and made the headlines, since his response was so unusual for a pope. "If someone is gay and he searches for the Lord and has good will, who am I to judge?" It was the first time a pope had used the word 'gay' to refer to a person with same-sex attraction, and he probably did so because that is how they refer to themselves. We all have desires that are disordered and that is why we sin. The Pope is conveying a strong message: who are we, the people, to judge if a person is tempted in a different way than we are? Priests are called to celibacy, and a priest with same-sex attraction is called to celibacy just as a priest who is attracted to the opposite sex. Currently, candidates for the priesthood may only have attraction for the opposite sex if they are to be ordained. If Pope Francis makes a change has yet to be seen, but what is clear is that Pope Francis sees homosexuality as a temptation to the person. Someone who is Catholic and gay and truly "searches for the Lord" will find that he or she must not act on those temptations, just as a heterosexual Catholic not in a Church marriage must not act on temptations regarding the opposite sex.

Pope Francis always tries to look first to the person. In his interview with Eugenio Scalfari of La Repubblica, an atheist, the journalist joked that his friends told him that the Pope only accepted the interview to convert him. Pope Francis responded, "Proselytism is solemn nonsense, it makes no sense. We need to get to know each other, listen to each other and improve our knowledge of the world around us." During the interview, the Holy Father did not hold back on sharing about the message of Jesus and even asked the journalist penetrating questions to lead him to recognize the truth. That is evangelization. While it was later noted that the elderly Scalfari did not take notes or record the interview and thus may not have recalled the wording correctly, the difference that Pope Francis highlighted between proselytism and evangelization is that proselytism is a preaching that does not consider the person, while true evangelization is a personalistic sharing of the Gospel message done with love.

Pope Francis applies the principle of mercy to atheists as he did when he was a cardinal. His approach to atheists is one of respect and of open arms. One of the Holy Father's spontaneous morning homilies at the Domus Sanctae Marthae, intended for the Vatican staff and their families, made headlines, "The Lord has redeemed all of us, all of us, with the Blood of Christ: all of us, not just Catholics. Everyone! 'Father, the atheists?' Even the atheists. Everyone! And this Blood makes us children of God of the first class. We are created children in the likeness of God and the Blood of Christ has redeemed us all. And we all have a duty to do good."

It is Catholic teaching that the mercy of God extends to all people and not just Catholics. According to Vatican II, "[The Church of Christ] constituted and organized in the world as a society, subsists in the Catholic Church... although many elements of sanctification and of truth are found outside of its visible structure. These elements, as gifts belonging to the Church of Christ, are forces impelling toward catholic unity" (from Lumen Gentium). A distinction might be made between redemption, which is offered to all, and salvation, which may not be received by all because of a lack of response to Christ's redemption. Those outside the bounds of the Catholic Church can be saved, but as the Congregation for the Doctrine of the Faith under Cardinal Ratzinger (the future Pope Benedict XVI) clarified in a document called 'Dominus Jesus,' it is presumably more difficult because the full elements towards salvation are in the Catholic Church.

Still, we are all children of the same God, whether we believe in him or not. We have much to share. All people of good will share in God's common gifts of goodness, truth, and beauty. Pope Francis continues, "And this commandment for everyone to do good, I think, is a beautiful path towards peace. If we, each doing our own part, if we do good to others, if we meet there, doing good, and we go slowly, gently, little by little, we will make that culture of encounter: We need that so much. We must meet one another doing good. 'But I don't believe, Father, I am an atheist!' But do good: We will meet one another there."

At his first meeting with the journalists on March 16, he modeled a respect for those of other faiths: "I told you I was cordially imparting my blessing. Since many of you are not members of the Catholic Church, and others are not believers, I cordially give the blessing silently, to each of you, respecting the conscience of each, but in the knowledge that each of you is a child of God. May God bless you!"

Church Reform

While Pope Francis has always been a strong advocate and sincere practitioner of social justice, he has stated on numerous occasions that the Church of Christ is not to be equated with an NGO (a nongovernmental organization), such as the Red Cross, UNICEF, or the United Way. While many NGO's perform good deeds, if the Church acted as another NGO, it would be a pitiful one because that is not its call and the reason for its existence. The Church is called to be the Bride of Christ. As a result, the Church pleases Christ by serving him in the poor. Pope Francis likewise keeps his distance from clericalism, in which the clergy assume privilege at the expense of the laity and lack a spirit of service. The Holy Father says that in meeting a clericalist, "I suddenly become anti-clerical." He is a strong believer in Vatican II's emphasis on the Church as all the people of God, served by their leaders in the clerical hierarchy. Hence Pope Francis told his priests on Holy Thursday that they must be "shepherds living with the smell of their sheep." And at his meeting with journalists on March 16 he said, "How I would like a Church which is poor and for the poor!"

Vatican II teaches that the Church is holy because Christ, her head, is holy. What people see of the institutional Church is often short of Christ's holiness because the Church and its leaders are made up of sinners. Pope Francis, too, identifies himself to the world as a sinner. Even the Pope is a sinner, and the Church's teaching on papal infallibility, limited to particular instances of teaching officially on faith and morals, has never denied that. Much like Jesus himself, Pope Francis is not afraid to make controversial statements to shake people, both believers and non-believers, from their comfort zone and change their paradigm of thought. For Pope Francis, the problem with the Church today is not its teachings or moral doctrines, but rather the members of the Church, and even many of the leaders, do not sufficiently practice what they preach. If the world saw Catholics truly living like they believed what they said they believed, then the world would have more respect for the Church when it teaches on abortion, homosexuality, or other such topics.

Pope Francis is not afraid to call out the Church on hypocrisy. He even brought up the topic of the sex abuse scandals on his own at World Youth Day, and has confronted the issue head-on during his time as a cardinal. Speaking not of the institution of the Curia itself, but of Vatican-centric cronies and bureaucrats, he told Eugenio Scalfari of La Repubblica, "Leaders of the Church have often been Narcissus, flattered and sickeningly excited by their courtiers. The court is the leprosy of the papacy." He continued in describing this attitude that must change, "It sees and looks after the interests of the Vatican, which are still, for the most part, temporal interests. This Vatican-centric view neglects the world around us. I do not share this view and I'll do everything I can to change it."

The Curia itself, as Pope Francis told Father Spadaro, is a necessary institution intended to assist the Pope. There are various congregations, such as on the Clergy, on the Faith, on Evangelization, on Bishops, on Justice and Peace, on Worship, and more. The Pope, as a single man, could never accomplish all the work on his own regarding situations throughout the world. The Curia has sometimes been reactionary and has had the tendency for centralization and institutionalization. Pope Francis has noted, for example, that many of the cases that come to the Congregation for the Doctrine of the Faith that concern matters of heterodox teachings could be much more suitably handled at the diocesan level.

Pope Francis has admitted that he does not fully know on his own what to do about all the problems of the Vatican, yet he is committed to learning more about the issues and seeking the proper reforms. His most effective leadership for reform is his example of humility, openness, and authenticity, for as he has said, the reform of the Church must first begin with the conversion of hearts. On April 13, Pope Francis, appointed eight cardinals to form a panel to look into how the Curia might be reformed to more effectively serve the Pope and the Church. Initially, Pope Francis kept the incumbents in the Curia, but after the summer he made a number of key changes. On August 31, he appointed Archbishop Pietro Parolin, a veteran Vatican diplomat, as Secretary of State in place of Cardinal Bertone.

Then, on September 21, he named new prefects of the Congregation for the Doctrine of the Faith and the Congregation for Evangelization. He also appointed a new Apostolic Penitentiary to oversee investigations regarding the sacrament of Reconciliation. He also appointed a new Secretary General for the Synod of Bishops to give the discussion among the bishops of the world a more prominent place within the Vatican. Pope Francis also has a special interest in reforming the Vatican Bank. He requires greater transparency in the institution and appointed an audit commission to monitor the corruption-prone bank. The Vatican Bank issued its first ever earnings report on October 1, 2013.

Pope Francis has emphasized that the focus of the Church must always be on Christ and that proclaiming the love of Christ is primary. Other doctrines of the Church follow the more fundamental ones. The General Directory for Catechesis, issued in 1997 by the Vatican Congregation for the Clergy, states that the Catholic faith "has a comprehensive hierarchical character, which constitutes a coherent and vital synthesis of the faith. This is organized around the mystery of the Most Holy Trinity, in a christocentric [or Christ-centered] perspective, because this is the source of all other mysteries of the faith, the light that enlightens them."

Recalling this hierarchy of truths, one in which more fundamental truths enlighten the others, Pope Francis told Father Spadaro, "We cannot insist only on issues related to abortion, gay marriage and the use of contraceptive methods. This is not possible. I have not spoken much about these things, and I was reprimanded for that. But when we speak about these issues, we have to talk about them in a context. The teaching of the church, for that matter, is clear and I am a son of the church, but it is not necessary to talk about these issues all the time. The dogmatic and moral teachings of the church are not all equivalent. The church's pastoral ministry cannot be obsessed with the transmission of a disjointed multitude of doctrines to be imposed insistently. Proclamation in a missionary style focuses on the essentials, on the necessary things: this is also what fascinates and attracts more, what makes the heart burn, as it did for the disciples at Emmaus." Pope Francis is not critiquing the Church's teachings on abortion or homosexuality. Instead, he is speaking about a clear presentation of the core Gospel message, without which, these teachings will fall on deaf ears. In fact, on May 12, Pope Francis had surprised over 40,000 people gathered for the Italian March for Life by personally joining them.

The topic of the role of women in the Church has been kept at the fore, especially in the media. Pope John Paul II wrote in his 1994 apostolic letter Ordinatio Sacerdotalis that "in order that all doubt may be removed regarding a matter of great importance... I declare that the Church has no authority whatsoever to confer priestly ordination on women and that this judgment is to be definitively held by all the Church's faithful." The Church, bound by Scripture and Tradition, finds no support in the message for women to be ordained as priests, and the fact that Christ himself chose only males for his Apostles reinforces this belief. Pope Francis confirmed that the ordination of women to the priesthood should not be considered. He told journalists on the plane to Rio that "with reference to the ordination of women, the Church has spoken and says, 'No.' John Paul II said it, but with a definitive formulation. That is closed, that door... But he has called on numerous occasions for a deeper theology of women in the Church." While women do hold many positions of authority within the Church and its institutions today, Pope Francis says the first question is not whether a woman may hold this position or that one.

He told the journalists, "No! It must be more, but profoundly more, also mystically more, with this that I said about the theology of the woman." Such a deepened theology of women in the Church must consider that while the Apostles were given the authority of the Church, Mary, the Mother of God, is still greater than they are for the life of the Church.

Pope Francis and the Youth

Pope Francis has struck a special chord with the youth. He has always been close with young people. He served many years as a secondary school teacher and later as a confessor and spiritual director popular among the youth when he was an auxiliary bishop. He understands them. The youth, and particularly the current generation, respect authenticity in a person's character. They are very sensitive to hypocrisy, respecting a genuine person even if they may disagree. Pope Francis offers young people authenticity, simplicity, action, and truth.

World Youth Day 2013 was scheduled through July 23-28, in Rio de Janeiro, Brazil. Prior to his resignation, it was not clear that Pope Benedict would be able to make the trip for the 28th World Youth Day because of his health. His doctors, in fact, had told him he could not take an international flight. By July 2013, as providence would have it, it would be Pope Francis' turn to celebrate the perennial celebration of the world's Catholic youth founded by Pope John Paul II. This time the celebration took place in Rio, which is in Pope Francis' native Latin America.

Having carried his own luggage onto Shepherd 1, the Alitalia plane used by the Pope and those traveling with him, Pope

Francis greeted the thousands of young people who came to the airport to welcome him on July 22, "I ask permission to come in and spend this week with you" (as reported in coverage by National Catholic Reporter). If Pope Francis needed an answer, he would soon find it. The popemobile, as it made its way to the presidential palace, had to take a detour as it slowly inched forward because of the crowds and congestion. Enthusiastic crowds took the opportunity to jump right in and lovingly surround the Holy Father's vehicle, hoping to touch him. While the papal security was alarmed, Pope Francis felt very much at home, shaking hands through the window and greeting well-wishers. To make for more security headaches, but to the delight of the crowds, Pope Francis had eschewed the popemobile, closed in by bulletproof glass, for an open-air white Jeep, just as he has opted for in Rome.

An hour late, Pope Francis finally reached the presidential palace. He expressed his joy to be back in Latin America, attributing it to God's "loving providence" that Pope Benedict had selected Rio for the event. Echoing St. Peter, he told the crowds, "I have neither silver nor gold, but I bring with me the most precious thing given to me: Jesus Christ!" Having visited the rich, Pope Francis did not forget the poor.

He headed later that day to the favelas, the slums that surround Rio's modern skyline, to spend time with the poorest in the city as he was accustomed to doing in Buenos Aires. He told them, "The Brazilian people, particularly the humblest among you, can offer the world a valuable lesson in solidarity, a word that is too often forgotten or silenced because it is uncomfortable."

On July 24, Pope Francis spoke to journalists about the problems faced by young people today. Recalling the lessons he learned on the value of work from his own youth, the Holy Father shared, "The young, at this time, are in a situation of crisis. We are somewhat accustomed to this culture of rejection: too often we discard the elderly. But now, also with the young unemployed, the culture of rejection reaches them too. We have to eliminate this habit of rejection!"

As a cardinal, Pope Francis, would often hear confessions at major events. He continued this practice; he joined his brother priests in hearing the confessions of young people at Quinta da Boa Vista Park in Rio, on July 26. After participating in a full schedule of events with the youth of the world gathered in Rio, Pope Francis was joined by over three million young people for Sunday Mass on the expansive beaches of Copacabana, a site more familiar with partying than papal services. He told the young people, recapping his homily, "Go, do not be afraid, and serve. If you follow these three ideas, you will experience that the one who evangelizes is evangelized, the one who transmits the joy of faith receives more joy." The Holy Father believes very much that the young people are the ones that will reach the most young people for Christ. The youth at Rio placed their trust in Pope Francis. When departing for Rome on July 29, Pope Francis told the youth, "I will always place my hopes in young people."

Pope Francis would meet again shortly with the youth. He gathered with about 20,000 young people outside Our Lady of the Angels Basilica in Assisi on October 4, towards the end of his celebration of the memorial of St. Francis. There, he answered a number of their questions. While the millennial generation has often been noted for its lack of commitment, Pope Francis told the young people not to be afraid: "I want to tell you not to be afraid of taking definitive steps in life." He told them, "I ask you, instead, to be revolutionaries, I ask you to swim against the tide; yes, I am asking you to rebel against this culture that sees everything as temporary and that ultimately believes you are incapable of responsibility - that believes you are incapable of true love. I have confidence in you and I pray for you. Have the courage to swim against the tide. And also have the courage to be happy." He explained that marriage and the priesthood are the kind of definitive commitments through which we find fulfillment. "One time I heard a good seminarian say: I want to become a priest for ten years. Then I will think about it again. That's the culture of provisionality. Jesus did not save us provisionally, he saved us definitively."

Pope Francis also encouraged the young people to see marriage as a true vocation, telling them, "It takes courage to start a family." He also denounced the culture of divorce which has increased in recent decades: "You know that marriage is for a lifetime? 'Yes, we love each other, but we'll stay together as long as love lasts. When it's over, we go our separate ways.' That is selfishness."

At the same time, Pope Francis has also expressed pastoral concern for Catholics who are divorced and remarried. It is a practice that is contrary to the Church's teachings, yet many Catholics find themselves today in that state and may not receive Communion. The Holy Father calls such persons to participate actively in parish life and to stay close to Christ. Meanwhile, Pope Francis called together his first extraordinary Synod of Bishops to meet in October 2014 to discuss the topic of family and marriage, an institution that is so essential to society, but remains in crisis.

Pope Francis' Role in the Church

Like an Old Testament prophet shaking believers and non-believers alike by his words and actions, Pope Francis continues to make headlines around the world nearly every day. He continues to apply the 'medicine of mercy' that Pope John XXIII called for at Vatican II in new and surprising situations. From the 'End of the World,' the Argentine Pope brings a new perspective on the traditional faith. He is carrying out his role as Supreme Teacher most eloquently through his gestures of love and mercy. He strikes a chord in the hearts of many that have been closed in the past to what the Church offered.

Pope Francis wants this medicine of mercy to reach everyone. He speaks of a 'holy middle class' that he wants to reach and foster. He tells Father Spadaro, "There is a 'holy middle class,' which we can all be part of... I see the holiness in the patience of the people of God: a woman who is raising children, a man who works to bring home the bread, the sick, the elderly priests who have so many wounds but have a smile on their faces because they served the Lord, the sisters who work hard and live a hidden sanctity. This is for me the common sanctity."

While Pope Francis has often been contrasted in the media with his predecessors, there is in fact much continuity. Pope Francis' changes are not intended as a rebuke to former popes, but are simply the way he has always ministered as a pastor. Cardinal Dolan tells us in "Praying in Rome", "Pope Francis is a simple and sincere man, not one scripting his actions and messages. He's just himself. This is who he is. He has no marketing plan that says, for instance, that he's not going to live in the papal apartments or that he's only going to speak in Italian. His strategy and protocol is his sincerity."

The three popes should be seen in a hermeneutic of continuity. Like Pope John Paul II, Pope Francis is a charismatic and open figure, comes from a far-away land, loves the youth, and has great devotion to Mary. Like the son of Poland, he is interested in a theology of women grounded in the example of the Blessed Virgin, has dealt with oppressive regimes, and speaks strongly from the Church's social teaching. In fact, Pope Francis has finalized and approved Blessed John Paul II's canonization as a saint, which he plans to preside over on April 27, 2014. Like Pope Benedict, Pope Francis has a love of the Church as the Bride of Christ, warns against reducing the Church to merely a nongovernmental organization, has zeal for social justice, and has a personal presence of humility. Pope Francis shared the following about his predecessor's resignation, "Pope Benedict has done an act of holiness, greatness, humility. He is a man of God." In fact, on June 29, Pope Francis promulgated the encyclical Lumen Fidei (The Light of Faith), which Pope Benedict had been working on as a catechesis for the Year of Faith and has added a number of his own touches as well.

The encyclical, which speaks eloquently in Pope Benedict's usual style on the harmony of faith and reason and the importance of faith for society as a whole, completes the series of encyclicals Pope Benedict had intended as a catechesis on the theological virtues: faith (Lumen Fidei in 2013), hope (Spes Salvi in 2007), and charity (Deus Caritas Est in 2005). Pope Francis visited with the Pope Emeritus at Castel Gandolfo on March 23, and in the Vatican Gardens on July 6, to converse and to pray. At Castel Gandolfo, Pope-Emeritus Benedict, dressed as he does now in a simple white cassock, attempted to show special deference to Pope Francis, to which the new Holy Father responded, "We are brothers."

In fact, some have even described the three pontificates in terms of the three theological virtues: hope for John Paul II, who encouraged the people from the Cold War through the Millennium to "be not afraid," faith for Pope Benedict XVI, who emphasized the unity of faith and reason, and charity for Pope Francis, who has put the teachings of his predecessors into practice in a dramatic and touching way. All three popes have worked successively to fully implement Vatican II. Pope Francis inherits from Pope John Paul II and Pope Benedict pastoral boundaries for the reform from Vatican II to retain continuity with the Church throughout the ages. All three popes have taught the same unchanging Faith of the Church.

Pope Francis tells us that despite the problems of the Church and the world, we should have hope for the future. On March 15, he told the College of Cardinals, "Never give in to the devil's pessimism, discouragement and bitterness. Christians need to share the Gospel message with joy and courage because it will truly answer people's deepest needs." The Holy Father explained to Father Spadaro that it is not optimism he is looking for. He says, "I do not like to use the word optimism because that is about a psychological attitude. I like to use the word hope instead.... The fathers of the faith kept walking, facing difficulties. And hope does not disappoint...." He continues, "Christian hope is not a ghost and it does not deceive. It is a theological virtue and therefore, ultimately, a gift from God that cannot be reduced to optimism, which is only human. God does not mislead hope; God cannot deny himself. God is all promise."

Today, many people are looking the Church to change. Some are looking for Pope Francis to change doctrines. Pope Francis has insisted that what needs to change is not the doctrines, which by their nature cannot change, but the people need to change. Cardinal Dolan speaks of the future changes in Pope Francis' papacy, "The Pope will call for a radical change within our hearts and souls, because that's what Jesus did. The Church is interested in a change in the human heart - a change otherwise known as repentance and conversion."

Pope Francis explains to Father Spadaro his approach to the problems of the Church of today, "The thing the church needs most today is the ability to heal wounds and to warm the hearts of the faithful; it needs nearness, proximity. I see the church as a field hospital after battle. You have to heal... wounds. Then we can talk about everything else."

The Rosary

The following section is written and compiled by the editor

In a September 2013 interview, Pope Francis discussed his daily prayers, stating, "I pray the breviary every morning. I like to pray with the psalms. Then, later, I celebrate Mass. I pray the Rosary. What I really prefer is adoration in the evening, even when I get distracted and think of other things, or even fall asleep praying. In the evening then, between seven and eight o'clock, I stay in front of the Blessed Sacrament for an hour in adoration. But I pray mentally even when I am waiting at the dentist or at other times of the day."

A month earlier, at the Mass for the Assumption of the Blessed Virgin Mary, Pope Francis urged Catholics to pray the rosary, "Mary joins us, she fights at our side. She supports Christians in the fight against the forces of evil. Especially through prayer, through the rosary. Hear me out, the rosary... Do you pray the Rosary each day? I don't know, are you sure? There we go!"

As a child, I remember seeing my grandmother pray the rosary. I remember thinking that the practice was odd, even frightening to watch. Often we are afraid of things that we do not understand, and I have since learned that the tradition of praying the rosary is quite beautiful. I hope the following chapter provides both instruction and reference for practicing Catholics, and a deeper understanding for those of different religions. The following chapter explains in detail the traditions of praying the rosary, a tradition that Pope Francis holds dear.

The following sections provide a brief overview of how to pray the rosary. This section also appears in The Life and Legacy of Pope John Paul II, by Wyatt North.

First, begin by holding the cross and repeating the "Sign of the Cross."

Sign of the Cross

In The Name of the Father and of the Son and of the Holy Spirit.

Then, "The Apostle's Creed" is said on the Cross.

The Apostle's Creed

I believe in God, the Father Almighty, Creator of heaven and earth and in Jesus Christ, His only Son, our Lord; Who was conceived by the Holy Spirit, born of the Virgin Mary, suffered under Pontius Pilate, was crucified, died, and was buried, He descended into hell; the third day He arose again from the dead; He ascended into Heaven, sitteth at the right hand of God, the Father Almighty, from thence He shall come to judge the living and the dead. I believe in the Holy Spirit, the Holy Catholic Church, the communion of saints, the forgiveness of sins, the resurrection of the body, and life everlasting. Amen.

Next, on the single bead just above the cross, pray the "Our Father." Remember, Rosary prayers are considered Meditative prayers as opposed to personal prayers. In personal prayer the prayer speaks to God. In meditative prayer we allow God to speak to us through his word and his Spirit.

Our Father

Our Father, Who art in Heaven, hallowed be Thy name; Thy Kingdom come, Thy will be done on earth as it is in Heaven. Give us this day our daily bread; and forgive us our trespasses as we forgive those who trespass against us; and lead us not into temptation, but deliver us from evil.   Amen.

The next cluster on the rosary has 3 beads. With this group of beads, the prayer should recite the "Hail Mary." The prayer should recite 3 Hail Marys while allowing God to speak through his words on the three divine virtues of faith, hope, and love.

Hail Mary

Hail Mary, full of grace, the Lord is with thee, blessed art thou amongst women and blessed is the fruit of thy womb, Jesus. Holy Mary Mother of God, pray for us sinners now and at the hour of our death. Amen.

Repeat this three times.

After the three beads, there is a chain. Hold the bare chain and recite the "Glory be to the Father" prayer.

Glory be to the Father

Glory be to the Father, the Son, and the Holy Spirit.

The next bead is a single bead. Hold this bead in your hand and say the divine mystery of contemplation. For example, if it were a Monday or a Saturday, you would say the first Joyful Mystery, "The Annunciation."

The First Joyful Mystery: The Annunciation of the Angel Gabriel to Mary (Lk 1:26-38)

In the sixth month, the angel Gabriel was sent from God to a town of Galilee called Nazareth, to a virgin betrothed to a man named Joseph, of the house of David, and the virgin's name was Mary. And coming to her, he said, "Hail, favored one! The Lord is with you." But she was greatly troubled at what was said and pondered what sort of greeting this might be. Then the angel said to her, "Do not be afraid, Mary, for you have found favor with God. Behold, you will conceive in your womb and bear a son, and you shall name him Jesus. He will be great and will be called Son of the Most High, and the Lord God will give him the throne of David his father, and he will rule over the house of Jacob forever, and of his kingdom there will be no end." But Mary said to the angel, "How can this be, since I have no relations with a man?" And the angel said to her in reply, "The Holy Spirit will come upon you, and the power of the Most High will overshadow you. Therefore the child to be born will be called holy, the Son of God. And behold, Elizabeth, your relative, has also conceived a son in her old age, and this is the sixth month for her who was called barren; for nothing will be impossible for God." Mary said, "Behold, I am the handmaid of the Lord. May it be done to me according to your word." Then the angel departed from her.

Then you may pray the "Our Father" prayer for the second time.

Our Father

Our Father, Who art in Heaven, hallowed be Thy name; Thy Kingdom come, Thy will be done on earth as it is in Heaven. Give us this day our daily bread; and forgive us our trespasses as we forgive those who trespass against us; and lead us not into temptation, but deliver us from evil.   Amen.

This brings you to a set of ten beads on the rosary. You should then pray 10 Hail Marys while contemplating the first mystery. The example of The Annunciation is provided above.

Hail Mary

Hail Mary, full of grace, the Lord is with thee, blessed art thou amongst women and blessed is the fruit of thy womb, Jesus. Holy Mary Mother of God, pray for us sinners now and at the hour of our death. Amen.

Repeat this ten times.

After the 10th Hail Mary you will have completed the first of 5 decades. The next section of the rosary, is a single bead. Repeat the "Glory be to the Father."

Glory be to the Father

Glory Be to the Father, the Son, and the Holy Spirit.

Next, on the same bead, pray the "O My Jesus."

O My Jesus

O My Jesus, have mercy on us. Forgive us our sins. Save us from the fires of hell. Take all souls into heaven, especially, those most in need of thy mercy. Amen.

Then, on the same bead, announce the next or second mystery. For example: if it is Monday and your praying the Joyful Mysteries, the second Joyful Mystery is The Visitation.

The Second Joyful Mystery: The Visitation of Mary to Elizabeth (Lk 1:39-50)

During those days Mary set out and traveled to the hill country in haste to a town of Judah, where she entered the house of Zechariah and greeted Elizabeth. When Elizabeth heard Mary's greeting, the infant leaped in her womb, and Elizabeth, filled with the Holy Spirit, cried out in a loud voice and said, "Most blessed are you among women, and blessed is the fruit of your womb. And how does this happen to me, that the mother of my Lord should come to me? For at the moment the sound of your greeting reached my ears, the infant in my womb leaped for joy. Blessed are you who believed that what was spoken to you by the Lord would be fulfilled." And Mary said: "My soul proclaims the greatness of the Lord; my spirit rejoices in God my savior. For he has looked upon his handmaid's lowliness; behold, from now on will all ages call me blessed. The Mighty One has done great things for me, and holy is his name. His mercy is from age to age to those who fear him...."

Next, repeat the "Our Father."

Our Father

Our Father, Who art in Heaven, hallowed be Thy name; Thy Kingdom come, Thy will be done on earth as it is in Heaven. Give us this day our daily bread; and forgive us our trespasses as we forgive those who trespass against us; and lead us not into temptation, but deliver us from evil.   Amen.

You will now come to the second group of 10 beads. You should pray 10 Hail Marys while contemplating the appropriate mystery.

Hail Mary

Hail Mary, full of grace, the Lord is with thee, blessed art thou amongst women and blessed is the fruit of thy womb, Jesus. Holy Mary Mother of God, pray for us sinners now and at the hour of our death. Amen.

Repeat this ten times.

You may now move on to each mystery, by repeating the cycle as illustrated above. Below are the remaining three joyful mysteries. Generally, The Joyful mysteries are meditated on Monday and Saturdays. The Five Sorrowful Mysteries are mediated on Tuesday & Friday, The Five Glorious Mysteries on Wednesday & Sunday, and The Five Luminous Mysteries on Thursday.

The Third Joyful Mystery: THE BIRTH OF OUR LORD (LK 2:1-14)

In those days a decree went out from Caesar Augustus that the whole world should be enrolled. This was the first enrollment, when Quirinius was governor of Syria. So all went to be enrolled, each to his own town. And Joseph too went up from Galilee from the town of Nazareth to Judea, to the city of David that is called Bethlehem, because he was of the house and family of David, to be enrolled with Mary, his betrothed, who was with child. While they were there, the time came for her to have her child, and she gave birth to her firstborn son. She wrapped him in swaddling clothes and laid him in a manger, because there was no room for them in the inn. Now there were shepherds in that region living in the fields and keeping the night watch over their flock. The angel of the Lord appeared to them and the glory of the Lord shone around them, and they were struck with great fear. The angel said to them, "Do not be afraid; for behold, I proclaim to you good news of great joy that will be for all the people. For today in the city of David a savior has been born for you who is Messiah and Lord. And this will be a sign for you: you will find an infant wrapped in swaddling clothes and lying in a manger." And suddenly there was a multitude of the heavenly host with the angel, praising God and saying: "Glory to God in the highest and on earth peace to those on whom his favor rests."

The Fourth Joyful Mystery: Presentation of Our Lord (Lk 2:22-35)

When the days were completed for their purification according to the law of Moses, they took him up to Jerusalem to present him to the Lord, just as it is written in the law of the Lord, "Every male that opens the womb shall be consecrated to the Lord," and to offer the sacrifice of "a pair of turtledoves or two young pigeons," in accordance with the dictate in the law of the Lord. Now there was a man in Jerusalem whose name was Simeon. This man was righteous and devout, awaiting the consolation of Israel, and the Holy Spirit was upon him. It had been revealed to him by the Holy Spirit that he should not see death before he had seen the Messiah of the Lord. He came in the Spirit into the temple; and when the parents brought in the child Jesus to perform the custom of the law in regard to him, he took him into his arms and blessed God, saying: "Now, Master, you may let your servant go in peace, according to your word, for my eyes have seen your salvation, which you prepared in sight of all the peoples, a light for revelation to the Gentiles, and glory for your people Israel." The child's father and mother were amazed at what was said about him; and Simeon blessed them and said to Mary his mother, "Behold, this child is destined for the fall and rise of many in Israel, and to be a sign that will be contradicted (and you yourself a sword will pierce) so that the thoughts of many hearts may be revealed."

The Fifth Joyful Mystery: The Finding of Our Lord in the Temple (Lk 2:41-52)

Each year his parents went to Jerusalem for the feast of Passover, and when he was twelve years old, they went up according to festival custom. After they had completed its days, as they were returning, the boy Jesus remained behind in Jerusalem, but his parents did not know it. Thinking that he was in the caravan, they journeyed for a day and looked for him among their relatives and acquaintances, but not finding him, they returned to Jerusalem to look for him. After three days they found him in the temple, sitting in the midst of the teachers, listening to them and asking them questions, and all who heard him were astounded at his understanding and his answers. When his parents saw him, they were astonished, and his mother said to him, "Son, why have you done this to us? Your father and I have been looking for you with great anxiety." And he said to them, "Why were you looking for me? Did you not know that I must be in my Father's house?" But they did not understand what he said to them. He went down with them and came to Nazareth, and was obedient to them; and his mother kept all these things in her heart. And Jesus advanced (in) wisdom and age and favor before God and man.

Additional prayers for the rosary are as follows:

LET US PRAY

O God, by the life, death and resurrection of Your only begotten Son, You purchased for us the rewards of eternal life; grant, we beseech You that while meditation on these mysteries of the Holy rosary, we may imitate what they contain and obtain what they promise. Through the same Christ our Lord. Amen.

FATIMA PRAYER

Most Holy Trinity - Father, Son, and Holy Spirit - I adore thee profoundly. I offer Thee the most precious Body, Blood, Soul and Divinity of Jesus Christ, present in all the tabernacles of the world, in reparation for the outrages, sacrileges and indifferences whereby He is offended. And through the infinite merits of His Most Sacred Heart and the Immaculate Heart of Mary, I beg of Thee the conversion of poor sinners.

MEMORARE

Remember, O most gracious Virgin Mary that never was it known that anyone who fled to Your protection, implored Your help, or sought Your intercession was left unaided. Inspired with this confidence, we fly to you, O Virgin of virgins, our Mother. To You we come; before You we stand, sinful and sorrowful. O Mother of the Word Incarnate, despise not our petitions, but in Your mercy, hear and answer us. Amen.

Chapter Excerpt from

The Life and Prayers of Pope John Paul II

As pope, John Paul looked to the words of Jesus to Peter, his predecessor, for guidance: "And when you have turned again, strengthen your brethren" (Luke 22:32). Toward that end, John Paul's first and ongoing efforts were to strengthen the members of the Church.

One of his first aims was to strengthen the family. Towards that end, at the beginning of his papacy, he organized his Wednesday general audiences into a series of 129 lectures organized around a single theme. This took place between September 1979 and November 1984. These homilies were later compiled and published as *The Theology of the Body*, which was, in part, an extended attempt to purge any residue of Gnostic distain for the human body. In these talks, he presented very carefully his view of family relations, elaborating what he had said earlier in his book, *Love and Responsibility*. Marriage was a vocation, just as the priesthood was a vocation, and fidelity was the core of both.

He included his explanation for why natural sexual relations, unimpeded by unnatural birth control interventions, was God's plan to uphold the human dignity of husband and wife. While he conceded that family planning was part of a responsible relationship, he argued that this could only take place through Church-approved, natural means of fertility regulation. Artificial means of birth control were, he argued, dehumanizing.

Another early focus was the priesthood. In 1979, on Holy Thursday (April 8), the day when priests renew their vows, he addressed a letter to every Catholic priest. The salutation read: "My Dear Brother Priests." His message was designed to reinvigorate their commitment to their vocations and to restore lost morale. Whereas Pope Paul had allowed more than 32,000 priests to be released from their vows, John Paul was going to make the process harder. He wanted his priests to recall why they had become priests and to recover that sense of purpose. He reminded them of the importance of their priestly celibacy, which is a gift of the Spirit, a renunciation for the sake of the kingdom of heaven. Through this renunciation, the priest becomes a man serving others and is thereby able to build up the Church.

As is well-known, the new pope very soon went traveling. He traveled more extensively than any pope before, going personally to speak with the faithful and encourage them. With targeted visits to Africa and Asia, he demonstrated the importance of youthful churches for the future. And while in

Africa, he deflected criticism about his many trips by suggesting that popes should take their cues not just from St. Peter but also from the peripatetic St. Paul. He didn't only speak to Catholics, however. One of his earliest trips brought him before the United Nations (October 1979), where in an hour-long address to the General Assembly, he lectured the nations of the world on human rights and human freedom.

Karol Wojtila had always believed the Church's core task was to proclaim God's love, mercy, and forgiveness. This was his vision as he assumed leadership of the Church, and he articulated it in his first three encyclicals as pope. He saw this as a joyous message and one that elevated the dignity of all human beings.

He knew very well that it was his task as pope to complete the implementation of Vatican II. Accordingly, he consistently looked to the Second Vatican Council for direction, particularly the conciliar statements on ecumenism, religious freedom, and the laity. He especially focused on *Gaudium et Spes* (see above) with its emphasis on the role of the church in the modern world, the dignity of the human person, and the community of mankind. The Church didn't need to be confined to church buildings; it had a role to play out and about in the modern world.

While Vatican II had begun the process of "declericalization," or adjusting the unbalanced emphasis on the clergy, it was John Paul who gave impetus to the effort. He wanted reemphasis on the Church as a community in which all the baptized are equally important. As such, there was room for a multiplicity of voices—women, young people, and various Catholic movements—to be heard within the overarching unity of the Trinity. The Trinity itself was the model for unity in diversity, and it was the foundation for John Paul's renewal efforts for the Church.

Made in the USA
Lexington, KY
10 July 2015